NUMBER NINETEEN
The Walter Prescott Webb Memorial Lectures

Essays on Walter Prescott Webb
and the Teaching of History

[THE WALTER PRESCOTT WEBB MEMORIAL LECTURES]

Essays on Walter Prescott Webb and the Teaching of History

BY JACQUES BARZUN, ELLIOTT WEST,
ANNE M. BUTLER, RICHARD A. BAKER,
DENNIS REINHARTZ

Introduction by GEORGE WOLFSKILL
Postscript by LLERENA FRIEND

Edited by DENNIS REINHARTZ
and STEPHEN E. MAIZLISH

Published for the University of Texas at Arlington by
Texas A&M University Press: College Station

Library of Congress Cataloging in Publication Data
Main entry under title:

Essays on Walter Prescott Webb and the teaching of history.

(The Walter Prescott Webb memorial lectures ; 19)
1. Webb, Walter Prescott, 1888–1963—Addresses, essays, lectures. 2. West
(U.S.)—Historiography—Addresses, essays, lectures. 3. History—Study and
teaching (Higher)—United States—Addresses, essays, lectures. I. Barzun,
Jacques, 1907–   . II. Reinhartz, Dennis. III. Maizlish, Stephen E., 1945–   . IV.
Series.
E175.5.W4E78 1985   907'.2024   85-4692
ISBN 0-89096-234-0

Manufactured in the United States of America
FIRST EDITION

To the Memory of Walter Rundell, Jr.

Contents

Preface

THE Walter Prescott Webb Memorial Lectures, held at the University of Texas at Arlington on March 15, 1984, form the basis of this volume. For nineteen years, the Arlington history department has sponsored an annual lecture series dedicated to the memory of Texas's most celebrated historian, Walter Prescott Webb. The theme of the 1984 lectures, "Walter Prescott Webb and the Teaching of History," highlights the impact Walter Webb had on the historical profession both as a teacher and as a writer. On only one other occasion since its establishment has this lecture series been devoted to an examination of Webb himself. The Department of History hopes that focusing attention once again on the man it has honored for nineteen years will make the contributions of this important scholar better understood and appreciated.

All the essays in this volume consider some aspect of Webb's legacy as a teacher. Jacques Barzun, professor emeritus at Columbia University, emphasizes Webb's philosophical and methodological contribution to the study of history. In his essay, Professor Barzun discusses in detail the direction historical studies have taken since Webb wrote. He argues that many of the so-called new histories could benefit from a return to the methods of historical inquiry practiced by Webb.

Elliott West, professor of history at the University of Arkansas, is concerned more directly with the historiographical issues raised by Webb's work and with the relationship of these issues to classroom instruction. His article carefully traces three dominant approaches to the teaching of western history, demonstrating clearly the significant impact Webb's ideas have had on the course of education in this field.

Anne Butler, assistant professor of History at Gallaudet Col-

lege, and Richard Baker, historian of the United States Senate, offer an appreciation of Walter Webb—the man, the historian, and
the teacher. Their unique style attempts to evoke a sense of Webb's
commitment to the teaching of history.

The authors of this contribution are presently engaged in completing a biography of Webb begun by their mentor, Walter Rundell, Jr. Professor Rundell died suddenly in 1982, and it is to him
that this volume is dedicated. Walter Rundell devoted much of his
career to analyzing Walter Webb's contribution to the historical
profession, so it is fitting that this volume, which pays tribute to
Webb the teacher, should be published in memory of Professor
Rundell.

Two contributors to this volume are from the Arlington campus. George Wolfskill, professor emeritus at Arlington, was a student of Walter Webb's and is a recognized authority on the New
Deal era. In his introduction, Professor Wolfskill combines his personal knowledge of Webb with his understanding of the issues
raised by the contributors to this volume. Dennis Reinhartz, asso-
ciate professor at Arlington, discusses the use of maps in the classroom. Throughout his career Walter Webb was committed to the
use of maps in education, so Professor Reinhartz's essay is especially appropriate.

Finally, as a postscript, Llerena Friend offers a personal tribute
to her mentor and colleague, Walter Webb. A recognized scholar
in her own right and author of a highly regarded biography of Sam
Houston, Dr. Friend brings together the words of Webb with those
of his eulogists to capture the essence of the man we honor with
this volume.

As editors our task was a simple one. We have merely as-
sembled the lectures; the credit for what you read belongs to the
authors alone. Credit for the lecture series itself belongs to C. B.
Smith of Austin, Texas, a student of Webb, whose kind generosity
has made this lecture series possible. As we approach the twentieth
anniversary of the series, our appreciation for Mr. Smith's devotion
to this event grows and deepens.

Sandra Myres, professor at Arlington and chair of the UTA history department's Webb Lecture Committee, deserves a special

thanks. For years it has been her commitment to the Walter Prescott Webb Memorial Lectures that has made them a success. Her creative energies have been an invaluable asset and we are all in her debt.

DENNIS REINHARTZ
STEPHEN E. MAIZLISH

Essays on Walter Prescott Webb
and the Teaching of History

Introduction

I was a visiting professor at the University of Texas during the spring semester of 1963. One morning in early March, Professor Walter Prescott Webb came by, and together we went over to the Radio/Television Department studio to preview a lecture in the "American Civilization by the Interpreters" series that Webb was producing with funds from the Ford Foundation. Later that morning, he and Terrell, his wife, left for San Antonio.

I drove to Arlington to spend the weekend with my family and was at dinner when a colleague called to tell me the news. Professor Webb, on his way back to Austin, had been killed in a one-car accident twelve miles south of Austin on Interstate Highway 35. Terrell had been critically injured but survived. The date was March 8, 1963.

I wept unashamedly.

In the fall of 1948, I enrolled in the doctoral program at the University of Texas specifically to work with Webb. Our association quickly became more a friendship than a student-teacher relationship, and I have often thought that what brought us together in the beginning was Webb's curiosity about my childhood background and what it had been like growing up in a tough, blue-collar neighborhood of a big city. In any event, Webb, as teacher and friend, influenced my career more than any other person, and even in death has remained an intellectual and moral force in my life. His picture hangs in my study; one of my sons, Andrew Webb Wolfskill, is named for him; my first book is dedicated to him.

In physical appearance Webb was hardly impressive. He was of average height, lean and slightly stooped, and he walked as if following a furrow in a plowed field. His ruddy complexion and bald head accentuated the watery blue eyes behind steel-rimmed glasses. It did not seem out of place that he smoked cigarettes.

He wore a Stetson hat the year around, and his suits, nondescript at best, always appeared rumpled. For years he wore a dreadful-looking overcoat. The weather was quite cool and blustery the morning that we went over to preview the film. As we left Garrison Hall, I asked, "What happened to the overcoat?" Webb blushed, looked somewhat sheepish, and with that crooked grin said, "Terrell made me get rid of it."

People who did not know Webb might have described him as aloof, maybe taciturn. Actually he was shy and ill at ease with strangers. Around women his manner became almost courtly. But when surrounded by friends, Webb was witty, a good conversationalist and story-teller, and his laughter, a brittle cackle, came easily and was a joy to hear. He was gentle and patient with students, probably to a fault. He was considered an easy touch in doctoral oral examinations. But he could flash anger and indignation at times, and when he did his language could make a sailor blush.

Webb, unlike some other stars in the historical profession, was both accessible and approachable. Celebrity status had come late in his life, and he had no illusions about it all. Whenever he was tempted to be impressed with himself, he would tell his seminars, he thought of what would happen if he stood outside the Gunter Hotel in San Antonio and asked people passing on the street if they had ever heard of Walter Prescott Webb. He did much of his writing in his office in Garrison Hall, and it was not uncommon to hear his old upright typewriter going late into the night. Over the years he developed a signal system. If the office door was closed, stay away; if it was slightly ajar, come in.

Webb was certainly not a historian and academician in the conventional sense. He did not much like to talk shop. Although he was elected president of both major historical associations, he did not like to go to professional meetings. He employed unorthodox research methods, and much of the criticism of Webb resulted from his practice of first developing a hypothesis and then gathering data to support it. To do this, his critics argued, was to do violence to the whole nature of historical research. Or, to put it in the neat aphorism of J. Frank Dobie, "Webb never lets facts stand in the way of truth."

Webb was an unconventional academician in yet another sense. He began his educational career as a public high school teacher, went on to be a principal, and, for a short time, was even a tennis coach. But he knew how to teach, and his reputation as a good teacher led to a position on the faculty at the University of Texas. In 1918, in a most unlikely turn of events, Webb was offered a post on the Austin campus teaching a course on how to teach history to high school students.

Much of his reputation as a classroom teacher was based on a technique he developed while at Cuero High School in Cuero, Texas. The technique was historical problem-solving by the use of both primary and secondary materials. The class thus became, in a sense, a community of scholars researching a topic and using the methodology of the historian. Webb summarized the details of this technique in a paper for the history section of the Texas State Teachers' Association meeting in Corpus Christi in November, 1915. The paper was published the next year in the *Texas History Teachers' Bulletin*. That same year, 1916, Webb moved on to the Main Avenue High School in San Antonio. The United States entered World War I in 1917, and that development prompted Webb to write an article entitled, "How the War Has Influenced History Teaching in San Antonio High Schools." In the spring of 1918, when the Department of History at the University of Texas decided to hire someone to train history teachers, Webb was a logical choice.

Webb not only had considerable success with his methods course, but over the years he also influenced the teaching of history through the publications of the Inter-Scholastic League, the Texas State Historical Association, and the *Junior Historian*. He had a section in the *Inter-Scholastic Leaguer* entitled, "Talks on Texas Books," which he used to emphasize the importance of state and regional history and the techniques for teaching both. For a time, in the 1920s, Webb collaborated with William E. Dodd, Eugene C. Barker, and others in the very successful *Our Nation* history text series. Throughout his career, Webb was concerned about history teaching in the public schools. As late as 1958, he was responsible for getting Ford Foundation funding to study the problems of teaching history in Texas public schools.

In the classroom, especially with the enormous increase in

class enrollments after World War II, Webb used the standard lecture method at which, quite frankly, he was not very good. He did not have a very good voice for public speaking and did not like to speak before large groups; he had a deliberate, dogged, matter-of-fact delivery which never strayed very far from his typed notes. Undergraduates who sometimes took Webb's classes because of his reputation were likely as not to come away disappointed.

But if Webb was unimpressive in the lecture hall, he was superb in a seminar, where he could use basically the same techniques that he had developed at Cuero. In his 1955 presidential address to the Mississippi Valley Historical Association in Saint Louis, he explained why his seminars were so successful:

> I speak now of my own experience with the seminar. In my entire life I have had only two ideas which I consider to have any originality. I am here tonight because I followed those ideas, without much regard for method, using that which would facilitate the pursuit. Each idea has resulted in a book. A new seminar was organized around each idea shortly after its arrival, maintained until the book was published, and then abandoned. No idea, no seminar.

A reputation in academe does not come about, however, because of skills in the classroom, and Webb was no exception to that rule. His reputation came from his writings, from four major books. *The Texas Rangers* was a local history; *Divided We Stand* was an intersectional study; *The Great Plains*, while regional in focus, had enormous national implications; and *The Great Frontier* was international in scope.

The Great Plains, published in 1931, was, of course, the most influential of Webb's books. In 1939, the Social Science Research Council selected it as the outstanding contribution to American history by an American historian since World War I. *The Great Plains* won him the Loubat Prize from Columbia University, was a finalist for the Pulitzer Prize, and was twice a Book-of-the Month Club selection. In 1952, it was selected by the Mississippi Valley Historical Association, forerunner to the present Organization of American Historians, as the most significant book in the first half of the twentieth century by a living American historian.

As his reputation grew, Webb became a visiting professor at a number of American universities as well as a Harkness Lecturer at the University of London and a Harmsworth Professor at Oxford. He was honored by his profession with the presidency of both the Mississippi Valley Historical Association and the American Historical Association. At the University of Texas he was given the title of distinguished professor and, in 1958, was chosen one of its four most distinguished living alumni. Since his death in 1963, Webb has been honored with an endowed chair at the University of Texas at Austin and the Walter Prescott Webb Memorial Lecture series which is now in its nineteenth year at the University of Texas at Arlington.

All of these honors were solely the result of Webb's writings. Yet here was another instance in which Webb was the unconventional academician, because his attitude toward writing was significantly different from most in his profession. In the first place, Webb insisted that a research project should be a major undertaking, should be a real challenge, should be, in short, worth doing. "I really want students who will write books," he once told an interviewer, "not those who are willing to stop with themes, theses, and dissertations." "A good book," he would tell his graduate students by way of explanation, "is worth a bale of articles." One result of this view was that Webb wrote comparatively few short pieces for the professional journals.

He also argued that history was a branch of literature and should therefore be written with imagination and feeling. He deplored the way most historians wrote, attributing much of the problem to their early training in graduate school. In 1955, Webb was asked by the editor of *American Heritage* to do an essay on how historians write. The essay was not published, because Webb's views were considered much too strong on the subject, and he was unwilling to tone them down:

> In graduate school the student is taught to select a subject of such small dimensions that it offers no challenge to the intellect, does not develop the mind, and has little or no significance when developed. He is encouraged to write without benefit of imagination, to avoid any statement based on perception and insight unless he can prove by the documents that his idea is not original. He is trained to be objective, and the best way to be objective is to be so colorless as to give the reader something akin to snow blindness.

Webb had such depth of feeling about writing at least in part because he considered historical writing another teaching tool, a means to learning and understanding, which should be addressed to the widest possible audience, not just to other historians. To write for other specialists in the field was simply "to whisper in each other's ear," as Webb put it. "What I wanted to be was a writer," he once confessed, "and I wanted to write not for the few but for the many, never for the specialist who doesn't read much anyway."

It is with Webb as a writer and with historical writing since Webb—that is, historical writing in roughly the last half century—that Professor Jacques Barzun's essay in this volume is concerned. *The Great Plains*, Barzun explains, marked a special date in historiography because in it Webb used new forms of evidence to explain a region and a large movement of population. Webb assumed that history must proceed from an original idea. Based on this assumption, he evolved his theory of history as the consequence of climate and institutional circumstances. He rejected the idea that history could be scientific; it is tentative, incomplete, and unscientific.

The key to understanding Webb the writer, as Barzun correctly points out, is the "original idea" that provided order and continuity to any amount of evidence and related "the patterns of forces, causes and effects that research discloses." Unlike the premise of the "Great Man" theory, history was not the conscious actions of individuals but their reaction to a common condition. From his "original idea" Webb was able to explain, in *The Great Frontier*, the development of a whole civilization in Western Europe.

What Webb wrote fits Barzun's definitions. History, according to Barzun, is "a narrative that sets forth a chain of motive, action, result, a tale of interaction between man and his environment at a particular time and place." The end product, good history, has special significance in that it helps to shape the mind of the reader "by providing it with vicarious experience . . . because in any slice of the past the experience is broader than any one person could master."

Barzun deplores the course of historical writing in more recent years just as Webb did. He concludes that many historians have given up writing history in favor of something else to which the name of history is falsely attached; it should be called "historical sociology" or "retrospective anthropology" or, in other cases, "psychiatry of the past." In other words, as Barzun so neatly puts it, what has been happening to the drama of history is that "the actors have been sent home and the scenery has taken over their parts."

Elliott West, in a delightful essay, analyzes a subject on which Webb had a profound effect, the teaching of western history. According to West, teachers usually approach the subject from one of three perspectives. One approach is to consider western history as a part of westward expansion, to treat it as part of an ongoing frontier process with heavy emphasis on the thesis of Frederick Jackson Turner. A second approach, the approach that is inherent in *The Great Plains*, is to treat western history as a geographical and historical account of a distinct region. A third approach is to consider Western history as myth. The Western myth which originally drew pioneers to the West and which continues to produce an almost endless stream of literary and artistic themes, has had a profound effect on how Americans see themselves and how the rest of the world sees America and Americans. While the third approach, the Western myth, has become increasingly popular in recent years, a check of United States history survey texts would indicate that, as an introduction to the West, the regional approach is probably the most common.

In their moving tribute, Professors Butler and Baker discuss a special dimension of the Webb legacy, his students. Their conclusion is that despite all else—his prize-winning books, his distinguished teaching posts, his many honors—it was Webb's "profound and lasting impact on his students that earns for him his deserved reputation as an educator of excellence."

Also included in this volume is a piece by Dennis Reinhartz. In his discussion of maps, Reinhartz highlights the Garrett map collection in the University of Texas at Arlington Library. Jenkins Garrett, a prominent Fort Worth attorney and donor of the Garrett Library and Map Collection, was a student of Professor Webb's. During the years that Webb worked on the *Our Nation* history series, part of his responsibility was to prepare the outline maps and map exercises that accompanied the texts. Webb's interest in cartography as a teaching tool is also quite evident in his works, particularly *The Great Plains* and in writings on water for Texas.

Webb viewed the writing, study, and teaching of history as not just an academic exercise, but as a solution for the problems of society. For Webb, history was not only an essential ingredient in the training of citizens and the education of people; it was also an instrument for social change that could, when properly prepared and used, improve society and better mankind's lot. The late Ray Billington once remarked upon Webb's "faith in the function of history as an irresistible persuader." Webb had the gift of being able to convey to his students, both in his classes and in his writings, that crucial significance of history. The essays in this volume are a testimony to that gift.

Walter Prescott Webb and the Fate of History

I am conscious of the high honor it is to deliver this memorial lecture in honor of Walter Prescott Webb, and conscious also of my inadequacy to the task as it might be ideally performed. For I am not an American historian, much less an historian of the West, the West that nurtured him and that he celebrated in the most perfect way, which is, by making it better understood. A colleague of mine, who knew Webb, has told me an anecdote that is in point here. They were discussing books on American history and Webb said, "Fred Paxson wrote a History of the Frontier—but he never really left Philadelphia."[1] Well, I have left New York, as you can see, but I'm very much afraid that if I talked of the frontier or the desert, Webb would say I was still at Rockefeller Center.

That is the reason why I have chosen to discuss an aspect of history that is not explicit but implicit in *The Great Plains* and *The Texas Rangers*. That subject was of concern to Webb—increasingly so toward the end of his life, as he reviewed his own achievement. It is a subject on which he expressed himself more than once at length and in detail. I refer to the nature of history itself: what is history, how should it be conceived and written? The subject is even wider—if I may say so—than the Great Plains; it is no one's predestined stamping ground; rather it is everybody's common ground, including—let me assure you—the nonhistorian, the ordinary citizen and reader of books.

To discuss the nature of history in one hour is of course impossible. I shall therefore confine myself to those questions that Webb raised or that are implied in his work; we are here first and last to think about him. He made his name with *The Great Plains*, which marks a date in historiography. Why? Because the book uses new kinds of evidence to explain a vast movement of population. Webb tells us that he had his great idea one night while he was still at work writing on traditional lines the history of the Texas Rangers.[2]

The great idea was this: two new things made possible the development of the semi-arid region he called the Great Plains. One was the Colt revolver; the other was barbed wire. The men who came out of the East passed from a forest region where the long gun, rail fences, and going about on foot sufficed to secure the means of livelihood. On the Great Plains, the size of the infertile territory required the horse, which in turn called for devices permitting self-defense and the handling of cattle without dismounting—the six-shooter, the lariat, and (for marking limits and raising pure-bred stock) barbed wire.

Armed with this idea, Webb spent a year in research, both to demonstrate that it fitted the facts and to discover what else had happened, what other changes in human life followed for Austin's colonists when, in Webb's words, they "crossed the environmental border" between the Eastern terrain and the plains where there is no wood and never enough water. Webb's first point about writing history is that it must proceed from an original idea. He congratulated himself on the fact that he had failed to get a Ph.D. at the University of Chicago and had never taken a course in the history of the West, so that he was saved from "parroting someone else's dogma" about the region he was studying. He was writing history, he said, "as I saw it from Texas," not from some center of learning.[3]

In that regard, he was certainly in one of the great traditions. From Herodotus and Thucydides to Macaulay, Parkman, and Lawrence of Arabia, notable histories have come from those intimate with the ground itself and the life upon it. Webb was sure that his preparation had begun at the age of four, when he heard tales of Indian raids and massacres and observed, albeit unconsciously, the climate and ways of life.

For his method of conscious study, Webb credited a maverick Canadian professor at the University of Texas, Lindley Miller Keasbey—the only instructor for whom Webb had any regard, and one whose later dismissal by the university confirmed Webb's lifelong contempt for the ways and purposes of academic institutions. Keasbey's formula for understanding society was to start from the environment as a base and build upon it, layer by layer, the elements and activities of civilization, all the way up to literature, which is its finest flower (I am again using Webb's own words, in condensed form).[4] During his search for evidence about the Great Plains, Webb regretted his lack of education, which forced him to study geology, geography, botany, and other subjects from scratch. But when he was done, with help from seminar students gratefully acknowledged, he considered the work much too fine to be used as a ready-made dissertation for the Ph.D. that his colleagues wanted him to have.[5]

From this first high achievement, Webb derived a theory of history as the product of climate and circumstance, a theory he extended later to account for the state of the nation in *Divided We Stand* and then to the world in *The Great Frontier*. But before going on to those extrapolations, I want to consider some of the bearings of the "original idea" on the writing of history. Webb explicitly rejected the claim of certain earlier historians that their work can be "scientific." Rather, he said, it is tentative, incomplete, unscientific.[6] True, the historian should be dispassionate, but he needs that "original idea" in order to relate in various patterns the "forces, causes, and effects" that his research discloses. And to "give meaning to the past," he "seeks out the one pattern for special attention." Let me reinforce this quotation with another: "I worked hard in books," says Webb, "to form a harmonious pattern which I knew beforehand was there."[7]

I am not troubled by the apparent inconsistency of "seeking the pattern" and "knowing beforehand it was there." What seems to me important is the combination of the environmental basis with the *one* pattern. He calls it elsewhere "the compelling unity of the American West."[8] Compulsion means causation, and the search for a single ultimate cause is modeled on scientific method. Science is said to explain when it has organized a mass of disparate phenomena as results of a single general force, operating uniformly in all directions. I think the same goal inspired Webb when he called his great idea the "key" to understanding the American West and when he wanted history to find in the past *an* explanation of *its* meaning.[9]

It seems to me also indicative that for Webb the root explanation was material—the soil and its climate. He attributed this postulate to Keasbey, as we saw, and later discovered that Keasbey had translated the work of an Italian, Achille Loria, who in 1895 had written a Marxist analysis of Capitalism in which land and its conditions play an explanatory role. Loria, curiously enough, is also cited by Frederick Jackson Turner in his famous essay on the influence of the frontier in American history, which Webb had not read when he wrote *The Great Plains*. What is even more curious is that neither Turner nor Webb seems to have known of Montesquieu's elaborate theory of land and climate in Books 15–18 of *The Spirit of Laws*, a best-seller of the year 1748.[10]

But in Montesquieu geography is shown as one condition of historical developments, not a sole cause.[11] The assumption of a sole cause, let me repeat, is a scientific idea—in particular, a principle of physics—which in the nineteenth century became an obsession in other fields than science. That is why Karl Marx, along with many other social theorists, looked for such a cause and all believed they had found it; that is why Darwin was celebrated as the discoverer of the single cause of evolution—and still is thought to have done so, although he himself acknowledged several causes. Darwin, it may be added, is one of the classic discoverers that Webb says he would wish to be ranked with.[12] Webb also discussed physics in comparison with history, regretting that experiment, which settles questions in the one, is not possible in the other.

The appeal of the single cause is linked with the conception of history as a vast process which overwhelms any individual will. The triumph of democracy in the last third of the nineteenth century certainly contributed to making that view prevail. It seemed self-evident when large anonymous masses migrated from Europe to America and within America to the West; it seemed confirmed when those same masses, by agitating and voting along geographical, regional, and social or economic lines, moved the nation in one direction or another. At such a spectacle historians gave up the earlier conception known as the Great Man theory of history, the idea which Emerson, for example, discussed in his essay on self-reliance and summed up in the dictum that "all history resolves itself very easily into the biography of a few stout and earnest persons."

These two preconceptions—of a single general cause and of resulting mass behavior—supported each other and led inevitably to the single cause being found in some material fact, such as the soil and its climate. The events of history could then be understood on a broad front, not as the conscious actions of individuals but as their reactions to a common condition. It followed that if the principle is sound, then by its extension to a wider territory, the development of a whole civilization could be explained; all its seemingly separate features would fall into place as outcomes of the underlying single cause. And since that cause continues to act, the future of the civilization may be predicted. This program of study and prediction—tantamount to science—is what Webb carried out in his second large work, *The Great Frontier*.

Now our concern with the nature of history requires that we leave Webb for a moment to glance at the debate about history-writing that was going on during the time of Webb's formative years and preparatory work. At the turn of the nineteenth century, the cultural currents I have mentioned—science, democracy, and the rapid transformation of nations and continents—were influencing the minds of historians everywhere, and notably in France and Germany. Dissatisfaction with earlier forms and methods was widespread, and new goals were proposed. Lamprecht in Germany (and also in Saint Louis, where he came as delegate to the Centennial of the Louisiana Purchase) preached the fusion of history with psychology and social science. Others, such as Max Weber, wanted to find the historical constants of a period or movement—physics again—and Weber started on its long journey the notion that Capitalism comes out of Protestantism. In his careful work, the Calvinist ethic is only one of seven conditions, but the later distortion by omitting the other six is characteristic of the desire to find the single cause. In Werner Sombart, the genesis of Capitalism becomes the identification of a single social type.

At the same time in France, a similar controversy raged for some twenty-five years, leading at last, in 1929, to the founding of a journal called *Annales d'Histoire Economique et Sociale* and to the publishing of a series of books under the general title of *The Evolution of Humanity*. The issue in the controversy was whether history should deal at all with persons and events or solely with material conditions and general states of mind. In these last two the concern is obviously—once again—with physical causes and with democratic or popular feeling. This group of French historians have been for half a century the models and inspiration for the majority of historians in every language;[13] their only competitors, fewer in number, have been the so-called psychohistorians, who have tried to be scientific in their own way, by digging below states of mind and material conditions to find in the unconscious the single cause at work in history.

What strikes one at the outset about the work of the French historians and their followers is that it banishes the individual from history. One man writes about "The Crowd from 1789 to 1848"; another gives us a "History of Prices and Incomes" during a certain period; a third describes in two volumes the feudal system of Western Europe without one vivid detail, one account of events, one living character—everything is abstract, deliberately so, in order to make possible comparison with other feudal systems. The result is surely like science in its complete lack of interest in particulars.

That feature tells us something more about the shift of history away from persons and events. The direction it moved in came from the pressure of sociology and psychology, as Lamprecht had wished. Here in the nineties were brand-new social sciences, using historical methods and gaining respectful attention to their findings. They and not history seemed to hold the key to what the public wanted, namely, explanations. These explanations had to do with the present; they told us about suicide, divorce, literacy, socialism, or crime. Historians, too, would have to discover explanations of important situations in the past. What did the Black Death accomplish? Well, it wiped out the Vikings in Iceland. Did it or did it not delay the discovery of America? The exact number of days' delay is unfortunately not ascertainable. We saw a moment ago how strongly Webb felt the pressure of this demand for explanations, "patterns of truth in the kaleidoscope."[14]

Another important element in creating the new history was one generally overlooked when people explain changes of ideas. I mean boredom, fatigue. The nineteenth century was the great age of history-writing; from the days of Scott and Ranke, the general public had been feeding on history insatiably, and by 1900 the young were tired of its contents—wars, politics, diplomacy, and the great figures dominating the great events. Research brought out more and more details about those same old things; it was time to look at something else. As early as 1895 in England, the influential historian Lord Acton advised: "Study a problem, not a period."[15] The intention was to undermine the dry-as-dust school of historiography which devoted itself to recording facts, large or small, and which considered a life well-spent if the scholar produced a monograph covering two years in eleventh-century Britain.[16] Those facts, moreover, were mainly political. Acton's suggestion to study problems would make room for ideas and attitudes and take the historian into the wider stream of life.

It was soon found that many kinds of documents existed, so far untouched and worth exploiting—county archives, private contracts, children's books, records of matriculation at colleges and universities, the police blotter in big cities, gravestones in cemeteries—a whole world of commonplace papers and relics to be organized into meanings. Such documents, moreover, told nothing important individually; they had to be classified and counted, which brought one nearer to science—theirs was a mass meaning, so to speak—and it brought one nearer to the life of the people; it satisfied the democratic feelings.

Such was the course of circumstance that led to the kind of study I regard as typical of our time: *Murdering Mothers: Infanticide in England and New England 1558–1803; Poverty and Welfare in Habsburg Spain; American Collegiate Populations; Madness, Anxiety, and Healing in 17th Century England; Fluctuations in the Prosperity of a Cloth-Making Town in Languedoc 1633–1789; A Prison of Expectations: The Family in Victorian Culture.* To complete the display and prepare the conclusions I want to draw, let me add a work of the second kind: *White Racism: A Psychohistory.*[17]

The first observation that occurs when one looks closer is that all these studies rely on the sampling method—poverty in Habsburg Spain has the subtitle: "The Example of Toledo." The prison which is marriage (or marriage which is prison) is depicted through the lives of five Victorian novelists. The madness and anxiety study is an analysis of the work of one astrologer-physician with a large practice. The next point to note is the limitation in Time. The accounts of infanticide and the cloth-making prosperity end, the one in 1803, the other in 1789. There is nothing inherently wrong with those spans and those sample cases except that each raises in the innocent reader the important question, What of it? Why should I read it?

Let us return to Webb for a possible answer. When he wrote a foreword to the *Texas County Histories*—a collection of 814 books and articles by different authors—he said: "The general historian who can synthesize them and tell the story of Texas with the same fidelity will have written the book that Texas is waiting for."[18] That is entirely sensible, for I would have you notice that he said the *story* of Texas. Now a story has a beginning, a middle, and an end; it has people with names, who act from recognizable motives toward an intelligible goal; and on the way to it, things happen: there are events: conflicts, disasters, triumphs, reverses, failures, creations, rejoicings, deaths, and rebirths.

Now think back to our collection of modern studies and ask yourselves, first, who or where Webb's "general historian" may be who will synthesize those fragments into the story of anything; and, supposing there is such a person, what chance there is that anybody will take him seriously when he disregards the prevailing conception of history and produces *a story*. In one of the current catalogues from which I took the titles of books just quoted, there is only one work with a title suggesting a story. It is *A Political and Diplomatic History of the United States*; it is by a Japanese, published by the University of Tokyo Press, and merely distributed by the American publisher.

From these several kinds of evidence I draw the conclusion that the twentieth century has given up the writing of history in favor of something else to which the name of history is falsely attached. The right name would be something like "historical sociology" or "retrospective anthropology" or in other cases "psychiatry of the past." The dominant concern is that of the social sciences, all of which, of course, can study only the past. When the past is recent, a mere couple of years back, nobody doubts that the work is sociology—for example, the Lynds' study of Middletown or the Kinsey Report on sexuality. Why should it be anything else when the subject is that cloth-making town in Languedoc or those marriages in Victorian times? A lecturer in history at the University of York has written *Crime in the 17th Century* by delving into the

court archives of the County of Essex. Thirty years ago Senator
Kefauver, as chairman of a committee investigating gangsterism,
produced a report entitled *Crime in America*; did anyone consider
him "an American historian"?[19] I submit that both men are sociol-
ogists. Neither has written a story combining men and events in
the foreground of a narrative, to which the "conditions" so important to Webb and our modern researchers are the background. In
other words, what has been happening to the drama of history is
that the actors have been sent home and the scenery has taken over
their parts.

   At this point certain doubts or objections probably occur to
you. One is: What does it matter whether a piece of work is called
history or sociology or something else? If it discusses an important
piece of reality in the past, surely it has value. That is true, with
some reservations. First, how reliable is the sampling—or more
exactly put, how trustworthy is the title? Describing Victorian marriage as a prison on the strength of the lives of five novelists seems
very risky. One of the five in the study is Samuel Butler, about
whom I know enough to be sure that his testimony about his parents is honest but strongly satirical, and fictional besides. More
generally, is it intellectually sound to take a handful of uncommon
characters and offer conclusions about a social institution over a
span of sixty-five years? As to other subjects, we should want to
know whether crime in one English county represents all the rest,
whether one town in Spain can tell us about poverty and welfare
throughout the peninsula.
   Just as important is the substance of these reports on narrow
local conditions. Can one imagine reading, remembering, and organizing in one's head these scattered data? One of the essential
features of history proper is that it is memorable—able to be remembered. Sociology, by its very nature, is not written to be remembered but consulted, usually for taking action. Statistical
tables, correlations of totals with years or with localities are important—and not memorable; they convey information rather than
understanding. They do not impress a pattern on the mind as history does when it *is* history, that is, a story, and not a social survey
backward in time. For a story has people, motives, and events nar-

rated in steady sequence—things which, when skillfully presented, the human mind imagines, re-enacts for itself and thus makes a permanent part of its memory. History provides a vicarious experience, as every novel does; a novel is a mock-up history.

Please do not suppose that I am against the contemporary practice of sociological excursions into the past. I would not stem the flood even if I could. My concern is to make clear that these books lack the form and the contents of history, are not "histories of" anything you can name; they do not affect the reader's mind in the permanent manner of true histories. In these conditions it seems reasonable to ask that such volumes be called something else. The public is entitled to correct designations, if only to find fairly easily what it wants when in search of history.

Someone may urge in rebuttal that no matter how these works deal with the past, their substance is by that very fact a part of history. This is true. A genuine historian is grateful for such studies when well done and will use any transferable conclusion in his narrative, as Webb hoped that the Texas county studies would contribute data for the history of the state. But when this quite traditional idea is proposed, one is met by blank stares. After which someone is kind enough to explain, in the tone used to a slow-witted child, that so much has been dug out by so many workers from the archives of towns and counties, courthouses and police stations, colleges and insane asylums that synthesis is impossible: no mind can grasp it all, no lifetime is long enough. Besides, the careful scholar would want to go back to the sources himself; each detail must be felt at first hand if it is to be put in its proper place in a vast design.

These statements are the best demonstration that scholarship is engaged in a self-defeating game. For if the preliminary studies are too numerous to be used and are distrusted besides, they are not preliminary to anything, except perhaps academic promotion within a department. Webb, being a scornful anti-academic, had an answer to this counsel of futility: he was sure that after absorbing and reflecting on a certain mass of facts, the gifted historian would be inspired with an "original idea" capable of organizing any amount of evidence. The original idea has to be tested, but there is no need to turn encyclopedic and run after every fact. The great histories, he pointed out, continue to be read despite accumulations of new facts, whereas the monographs, unless useful to a great historian, remain only a professional exercise.[20]

But there is yet a third objection to the demand for history proper: being a narrative, it presupposes men and women whose motives lead to action and result in events. And we no longer believe in the importance, even in the reality, of active men and women. We think they are moved by other forces of which they are not conscious—by economic, dialectic, material determinism; or by a thing called "their society" (or culture); or by the unconscious, individual or collective; or, as Webb decided, by the environment. In all these accounts of the motive power *behind* history, we are back at the mercy of the single cause. For it is evident that no matter how much a theorist hedges by admitting lesser or secondary causes, the one he calls principal or fundamental is the one that drives the human crowd and commands the march of events.

The idea sounds so plausible: in an age of political democracy and mass culture, of world trade and interlocking industries, how *can* one believe in the Great Man and his directing will? The answer is, no need to believe in him, even though one has actually seen a few such rather recently—Stalin, Mussolini, Hitler, De Gaulle. But leave them aside and forget the label "great." The question is not that of supreme power, and not even of power, but of action. When Webb attributed part of the explanation of the West to the Colt revolver, he was giving a role to an object that would not have existed without a man—Samuel Colt. There was nothing casual about the success of the invention. Little Sam Colt was keen about guns and explosives from his boyhood. His early design and business failed, and he very nearly gave up. He persevered, helped by the onset of the Mexican War, and as a composite result of man and event, one of Webb's conditions was created. Nothing was inevitable, nothing fated in the sequence. Let me repeat: it took numerous acts of intelligence and will on the part of Colt and his backers before the weapon was produced in the East, far from Texas, and became as it were artificially part of the western environment. Revolvers do not grow in the desert like cactus, nor do barbed wire and windmills.

If it is argued that the environment produces the men who produce the devices, the generality is so indefinite that it explains nothing. To be sure, some environment and its culture, in the East, acted on Samuel Colt, but that setting had existed well before him and had not yielded a firearm usable in the West. Suddenly, in the sixth century A.D.., the desert of Arabia produced Mohammed, but no visible necessity called for his appearance, the results of which down to our time have been incalculable. The presence or absence of certain human beings makes a difference—Joan of Arc by her actions crowned a king and helped unite a nation. Suppose William the Conqueror killed at Hastings instead of his horse; the Normans had no other leader of ability. Now leave out, if you like, all future English history, Parliament, the common law, and just think of the English language; it is inconceivable that without the Norman Conquest it would have been what it is today; soil and climate did not do it all—and perhaps did very little. Individuals make a difference, though not wholly by themselves. Chance and will set the boundaries of human action, which in turn is hindered or favored by the particular scene. A true history is the tale of their continuous interaction at a particular time and place.

From that definition it follows that a history tells of particulars, concrete things, including persons. Sociology, on the contrary, and the social surveys that have latterly been taken for history, deal with abstractions—crime, poverty, marriage, income levels. Individuals do not count there; or rather, they are counted as interchangeable units and immediately forgotten so as to present a generality about the abstract condition: crime was high, prices were low, anxiety was rife. These truths may well be interesting, but they are static, and meant to be so; whereas history moves. We say "the pageant of history"; it would be absurd to say "the pageant of divorce statistics."

In pointing out the contrast between the concrete particulars of history and the abstractions of social science I do not mean to deny the profound appeal of generalities. It is normal and indeed necessary for the mind to seek meanings, and these usually take the form of general statements. We are bewildered by the welter of items in experience and want general, portable truths about them; for example, "clouds bring rain." We then say that we have the "explanation" of the facts.

Students of history are especially liable to this feeling of bewil-

derment and this desire to find an explanation. Webb's account of
the Great Plains was the fulfillment of that desire. And we know
that he went further and looked for the corresponding "key" to the
entire course of western civilization since 1500. He found it in the
effect on Europe of what he called *The Great Frontier*. The thesis,
set forth in his book of that title, is this: the western hemisphere
and its vast material resources formed a great frontier for Europe.
As long as riches were abundant, western civilization thrived and
was profuse in all kinds of creation, including the cultural. But by
1900 the frontier was beginning to close and shortly the door would
be permanently shut, with no other open frontier in view.

There is no need here to enumerate the difficulties, large and
small, that stand in the way of accepting this hypothesis. One thing
is clear. Webb's method, derived from Keasbey, of building the historical structure layer by layer, from the material base up to the
fine arts, is not carried out in this book with sufficient familiarity
with the tone and character of Europe itself, the complexity of its
history and of its leading figures. The treatment of economics at the
base and of literature at the top are notably lacking in sureness of
handling. Webb was out of his element, displaced from the post of
vantage he so rightly valued when he discussed the genesis of his
masterpiece. That first subject, he said, he had seen from inside;
the West was for him an ideal region because it contained "no industry, no special institutions, no battlefields, no statesmen—only
local politics, which are the least complex."[21]

Yet *The Great Frontier* also belongs in a discussion of what
history is, exemplifying as it does the urge to frame a philosophy of
history. An explanation of the past, said Webb, must supply its
meaning.[22] That conviction has produced a number of famous
works, from St. Augustine to Hegel and from Spengler to Toynbee,
whose *Study of History*, by the way, Webb seems to have regarded
with sympathy. But philosophies of history are not history, except
here and there, when the author narrates events to prove his thesis. To put it differently, the search for the meaning of the past
corresponds to the search for the single cause. They are the two
facets of one idea which is inherently antihistorical.

For a philosophy, a meaning, is by definition a principle that
does not accommodate exceptions. It is like a stencil laid over the

stream of events: only what shows through the holes can have significance, and unfortunately it is inevitable that what the stencil shuts out is often more important than what the philosopher needs to prove his principle, his meaning. Does this imply that history is meaningless? If so, what about the "original idea" that comes to the student as it did to Webb, enabling him to organize the confusion of the past? The difference between *an* idea and *the* meaning is twofold. First, the organizing idea serves for a modest portion of the past, modest in geographical range or in timespan. There is then no need to suppress or belittle great chunks of reality. Next, the bearing of an idea need not be exclusive; it may be offered as highly suggestive; it is a pragmatic explanation, in the technical sense of *pragmatic*. It is a view, a convenient pattern, a tenable interpretation, not a system or a stencil.

This second difference enables both the historian and the reader to feel free. The historian as he goes along does not need to stuff everything he finds into a set of prepared cubbyholes, and the reader can enjoy what he reads without the suspicion that he is receiving a garbled message. Thus to take two cognate examples, Gibbon can affirm that the decline of the Roman Empire was due to Christianity, and Mommsen can show how disastrous for the Roman heritage Caesar's assassination was. No damage follows to either of those historical masterpieces; the reader does not feel his mind coerced by a peremptory decision excluding all others.

My purpose in referring to the famous historians is to reach at last one of Webb's most important concerns, the relation of the historian to the public. With his rooted hostility to the purely academic, he insisted on the importance of readable history. Most of the history that is published by the professionals is addressed to the scholars in the same field and written in a style calculated to dispel any suspicion of wishing to attract. As Webb put it more explicitly, "One finds in them little charm, few vivid figures of speech, and practically none of that soft luminosity—an indefinable quality— which suffuses good writing."[23] In short, the past must be retold with art if the books about it are not to gather dust on the shelves of university libraries, taken down only by a few students working toward degrees. Webb deplored this divorce in our time between the historian and the general reader. He credits a few of the non-

professionals with having bridged the gap, but thinks these exceptions not enough—not enough for what? That question he answers
very briefly: the public does not get the explanations it should
have, does not understand the meaning of the past it might be interested in.

I think that this statement of the purpose of history writing
does not go far enough, and I shall try to give a fuller one before I
am through. Webb seems to have imagined a public naturally interested in the same enterprise as he and his students; he spoke of
himself and them as "an exploring party into an unknown country."[24] Such a safari is very enjoyable, as many of us here know, but
it argues a special rather than a general interest in history. It is like
the interest of poets in verse forms or of any artist in the technique
of his art. The public, on the contrary, is interested in the result—
the poem, music, or painting—and rightly so.

As for the "explanation" or the "meaning" of the past, we saw a
moment ago how thin and abstract such a thing is. Toynbee can be
summed up as having decided that there are twenty-one civilizations and that they were tested for survival by "challenge and response." Why read six volumes to find that out? The truth is that
when the great Toynbee boom occurred, twenty-five years ago,
more people bought the books than read them. Among the friends
of mine who are not historians, few finished reading even the two
volumes of the abridgement. Similarly, Spengler was understood
from his title alone—*The Decline of the West*—plus, perhaps, his
definition of Faustian Man, which anyone could learn from a good
review of the work. The mere explanation in Webb's *Great Plains*
is even easier to reduce to a formula, but fortunately his descriptive
power and love of the region and its people make the work much
more than the proof of a thesis.

Periodically, one of the abstract explanations gains wide publicity, either because it is startling or because the professionals praise
and attack it. But what other, closer contact has the educated person of our century with history? At times, a subject, the massive
research on which it rests, and some original feature about it draw
attention to a work classed as history. Most recently, for example,
Theodore Zeldin, an Oxford scholar, brought out a two-volume
work entitled *France: 1848–1945*. It took eighteen years to produce

and it seems to offer something new. The chapter headings certainly sound unusual; for example: Ambition; Marriage and Morals; Politics; Children; and so on. The author tells us at the outset that he wants to present "the permanent features of French society, to counterbalance the study of events."[25] The chapters contain social facts, anecdotes, quotations from books, and other items gathered from sources ranging in date from 1848 to 1945. They are loosely tied to a few working hypotheses; ambition, for instance, is supposed to be represented by six bourgeois occupations. The text is dotted with such remarks as, "It is difficult to attribute influence or cohesion to [these occupations] in any simple sense."[26] As for the ambitions of ordinary men, we are told, "they are unrecorded and difficult to write about."[27] On the relations involved in marriage, "they are even more difficult to trace than what a husband expected from a wife. The answers throughout the period are varied."[28]

All in all, it is most discouraging reading. There are no guideposts, no lines of continuity. A marriage manual written in 1806 is quoted next to one of 1883, followed by a public opinion poll of 1947.[29] Who can believe that these data all stand on the same footing, when nobody knows anything about the authors of those undistinguished books or the quality of the recent survey? By the end—I will not say of one chapter, but of ten pages—one is completely at sea as to any "permanent features" of French society; the bits and pieces are adrift in a stretch of one hundred years, during which it is not believable that marriage, morals, children, or the professions remained the same.

Yet this painstaking work has received high praise from the reviewers, no doubt because it answers to the prevailing idea of history, which I characterized as sociology of the past. I believe also that the form which for my part I found objectionable—the bits and pieces, as I termed them—is rather congenial to the modern mind. Is not television mostly bits and pieces that we assemble as we please, or even allow to flow over us unassembled?

Between Toynbee and Zeldin, the only work called history that has received general acclaim is Fernand Braudel's large study of the Mediterranean world. It fulfills the specifications of the *Annales* group by being quantitative about economic and social facts over a long stretch of time and territory and it does present patterns. But the figures and conclusions cannot be called memorable. They impress us, as a sympathetic reviewer said, only because we yield to the rhetoric of numbers. But all the work tells us was known before, much more agreeably, from traditional literary sources.[30] In a more recent volume, Braudel's way with history has been challenged by a critic who is evidently an historian:

> The mistakes and distortions which abound in Braudel's work are not so much incidental as inherent in his method, in his very approach to historical studies. For he will identify his long and medium-term patterns and cycles irrespective of events and policies, of political and military power. What confronts us in Braudel is a systematic disregard of the action of statesmen and the impact of alliances, treaties, and blockades. Occasionally, he stumbles awkwardly up against the fatal contradictions in his own method.[31]

We catch a glimpse here of what might be called the inhumanity or anti-humanity of that method. It professes to deal with populations and states of mind, but by eliminating from the account the varying fortunes of individuals and businesses, of soldiers, statesmen, and diplomats, it presupposes under the surface of things the action of a great machine; it is the automation of history.

In another genre which is not history but related to it, biography—a genre extremely popular today—one would expect individuality to have full and free rein. Yet the psychohistorians have managed, on the one hand, to trivialize destinies and passions through clinical conjecture, and on the other to mechanize the course of events by the operation of the unconscious force they describe. Meanwhile, in the most popular style of writing lives, the reader is likely to miss order and pattern. Such a book, to be adequately fat and sell widely, must consist of a mass of small details about domestic habits, furnishings, local life, neighbors, all loosely held together by condescension and obvious judgments. The more recent figures so treated are further loaded down with gossip gathered from surviving relatives, friends, and enemies. The repositories of so-called oral history are stockpiles of this kind of material, which should supply bits and pieces for biographers long after oil and natural gas have been exhausted.

It is important to remember that biography is not history; biography necessarily warps the fabric of history by the special prominence it assigns to the foreground figure. Yet today I think that the one kind of work likely to give the reader an inkling of history proper is the autobiography of the statesman or military commander, for it is bound to be narrative and to depict something of the confused interaction of many human beings and the role of accident. Such a book as Dean Acheson's memoirs, *Present at the Creation*, is a first-rate example of what I mean.

Despite this great dearth of history proper in our general reading, it remains true that the educated in the western world continue to respect the idea of history. They have forgotten the point of it, lost the feel for it, or they would not prefer sociology and philosophy or tolerate in the schools the dilution of history with "social studies." Yet away from books and from schools, the public responds to various kinds of appeals made in the name of history. For example, never have people celebrated anniversaries so incessantly. If it is not the village bank, it is the city department store, or NASA, or some literary periodical. Though democratic equality is not supposed to make much of family descent, there has been lately a great surge of enthusiasm for genealogy. Many people talk of their search for roots—a pastime as well as a source of self-confidence and pride. Meanwhile we record and collect every scrap and every object that suggests the past. Bringing up the anchor of the Monitor is called "a piece of the Civil War." Someone was even keen and bold enough about mementos to snip two inches from the hair of the Abolitionist John Brown, which was on display in the West Virginia capitol.

But again, all these things are only bits and pieces, even when the pieces are quite large, like the old sunken ships that various groups toil to raise from the seabed, or the "Historic Floor" of the Texas School Book Depository in Dallas, from which President Kennedy was shot, and which is being restored and decorated at a cost of three million dollars. In most cities a landmarks commission is busy saving old houses, as the National Trust for Historic Preservation does over the whole territory. The Rockefellers restored Williamsburg; and Henry Ford, who said "History is bunk," renovated the Wayside Inn and "Greenfield Village," Michigan, where the buildings and artifacts form a hodgepodge that defies the historical sense and include items of Americana imported from England.

This hop, skip, and jump relation to history is not wicked in itself, but it probably stands in the way of a genuine and sustained interest in history. A person who regards an historical object as a memento or a custom as "quaint," who keeps saying "in those days," or uses terms such as *Victorian, bourgeois, medieval* to signify traits that mankind has now got over is a poor prospect for the History Book Club. So true is this that the club itself is sparing in its proffer of *histories* and supplies as many, if not more, biographies and sociological studies.

The lack of historical "feel" goes with a lack of *feeling*, as shown, for example, in this country's willingness to have Memorial Day and other anniversaries moved about for the pleasure of a longer weekend. The Sunday paper announces, "Washington's birthday—actually February 22nd—will be observed on Monday." Our loss of historical conscience is in that word *actually*. The only thing observed on the Monday is the holiday parking rules. It is not celebration of great deeds or of the great dead to celebrate them when we are good and ready, putting convenience above the respect that the date should command.

If it were not for these distractions and derelictions, the least educated historical consciousness would rebel against the malpractice of those who make docudramas. The very word testifies against them. Even when they do not libel individuals, they present with all the force of "seeing is believing" a travesty both of what happened and of what could conceivably happen. Nor is the fraud perpetrated on the uninformed and uneducated alone. If the educated possessed historical awareness they would not debate in the public press the question whether Leonardo Da Vinci was or was not a pacifist. It is a case of "the question does not arise." But with the present atrophied sense of the past, a thing has only to be labeled old, or recorded, and it is believed to make its surroundings "historic." Like the taped interview or reminiscence, the raising and nurturing of presidential libraries has taught us to take the thing for the thought, so much so that some months ago the State of New York made the first move toward governors' libraries by appropriating three-quarters of a million dollars to publish ex-Governor Hugh Carey's papers in ten volumes. Objections on the ground of the economy were rebutted by historians, and Mr. Carey himself said that cancellation would be unfortunate, not for him but "for a sense of history downrange."

That public-spirited phrase unwittingly makes the point. A moment's thought will convince anybody that printing the governor's papers will contribute nothing to *a sense of history*. A sense of history does not reside in any set of bound books. It is something in someone's head; and that something, though born of natural curiosity, has to be cultivated in a certain way, by reading genuine history. Let me say once again what recognized, acknowledged historians have always understood by genuine history: it is a narrative that sets forth a chain of motive, action, result. The sequence in time—chronology—must be clear.[32] Dates are important solely for this purpose of orientation in the stream of motives, actions, results. The chain need not be long—Macaulay's *History* covers only twelve years—but it must be thick, for the motives and actions, being those of many individuals, are always tangled, and the results cannot be understood unless a full view of that preceding tangle is given.

Right here is found the value of history; not in some explanation reducible to a couple of sentences and even less in some powerful principle governing one or twenty-one civilizations. The value of history lies in the spectacle itself, the tangle and its results, called events. Reading history arouses and develops that "sense of history downrange" which Governor Carey wishes to promote. It gives a knowledge of how things go; it teaches what has been called the logic of events, which is not really a logic but a cultivated intuition of the probable in given situations.

This intuition is the only "lesson" of history, but it is of great worth, and learning it from good histories is enjoyable, since it means getting to know unfamiliar persons and their destinies in story form. When we speak admiringly of someone who has a vast experience of men and affairs, we are acknowledging what such experience does to a good mind; it gradually shapes that mind into an instrument for understanding the human world directly, without formulas, virtually without conscious thought. Exactly so does the reading of history shape the mind by providing it with vicarious experience. Because in any slice of the past, the recoverable experience is broader than one person could master, it has to be sifted and organized by the historian for the reader to grasp. Patterns and explanations have no other purpose, which is why they must remain conveniences, leaving the reader free to reinterpret the plot and to read other historians with different perspectives on the same subject.

On this view of history, the true role of books and studies on static conditions becomes clear. They are essential to the narrative historian when he comes to describe the setting, the material possibilities, the prevailing habits—in a word, the frame within which action took place. Obviously, the sense of how things go will yield different ideas when the piece of history comes from ancient Rome, from nineteenth-century China, or from the United States in the 1920s. Therefore, these various settings and limits must be made plain and coherently set forth; unconnected, inconsecutive bits and pieces will not help. Webb's great work has this indispensable merit of clarity, coherence, and consecutiveness, which is what puts it above so much of the would-be social history I have discussed.

Nor is this all. The historian who studies settings for his narrative or makes use of existing descriptions must choose a subject that is capable of treatment by pattern and chronology. That is why the political life of nations has been the most usual subject of histories. The chain is unmistakably there. It is possible to deal with aspects—diplomatic or economic history—or with single activities provided they are continuous—the history of baseball or of the fine arts. But topics that lack a spatial and chronological unity, such as "the history of the Irish in America" or "the history of Asia" do not yield books of history. The former subject has no continuity, the latter has no unity. On the same principle, there can be a history of feminism but not "a history of women." When the late Philippe Ariès wrote *Centuries of Childhood*, he supplied interesting vignettes of changing attitudes toward children, but he did not perform the impossible task of writing a "history of children," any more than he could have written the history of redheaded people: no links among them could be found; the chain would be missing. At the cost of a little repetition let me make this fundamental truth as clear as possible. A history could be written of the weather in Tarrant County between any two dates, but not a history of the thunderstorms. A History of the Idea of Progress is possible and has in fact been written, whereas a History of Human Stupidity cannot be, plentiful as the source material obviously is.

When as a result of the poor teaching in the schools, the withdrawal of professional historians from the literary scene, and the confusion arising from the replacement of history by social studies and social science the people as a whole lack the historical sense, it is not surprising that they wonder what history is good for. The backward vision of memorable images is for them not enough. History books, they complain, are not science but, as Webb recognized, uncertain and tentative. These questioners remain doubtful when one answers that history is exercise for the mind almost as good as golf is for the body. At the same time, it is amusing to note how often these same people will come out, in print or conversation, with Santayana's tag about those who forget their history being compelled to repeat it. There is a glimmer of understanding there, and perhaps a hope that quoting the words will help to escape the danger. No doubt it is assumed that in a specialized society the historians in their cubicles are doing what is needed. They are gathering and storing the information required to save us.

Such a belief is only another proof of the prevailing misconceptions. The statesman or diplomat who wants to avoid repeating mistakes cannot simply consult a book of facts or telephone an expert at a university to "get the dope" on a problem. He must possess history on his own account and long before the crisis. The words of the late Garrett Mattingly, a true historian, are relevant here. He said that to be useful, the past must be "brought into the full focus of consciousness, by a process similar to recognition."[33] That implies familiarity and a mind already formed historically. That is why I prefer to Santayana's rather mechanical recipe Burckhardt's great reason for historical studies: "not to be cleverer the next time, but wiser for ever." How far our governors are from this wisdom may be gauged from the recent remark of a Washington reporter about his stamping ground. It is, he said, "a city so obsessed with the present that anyone who can remember the Eisenhower administration is viewed as understanding the full sweep of human history."[34]

Yet in that very setting, that very city, some practical minds have tried to go against the current and explain the unique worth of historical knowledge, which is not a method but a form of thought. The distinguished diplomat Abba Eban was once interviewed about the new teaching of international relations through the "analysis of policy." He did not mince words; he said: "I don't really think it can compare with the vivid, living spectacle of history. And if . . . for any reason one had to sacrifice something, I would prefer to sacrifice the somewhat abstract jargon of these analyses, rather than . . . the direct contemplation of predicaments in which nations have found themselves and out of which they have emerged." In case the interviewer had missed the point, Eban came back to it: "I still believe that history, by which I mean the narration of situations . . . is a much more fruitful background than the algebraic formulas. . . . I don't think they can be a substitute for the deeply human contents of historical studies."[35]

To this recommendation there is but one short word to add. Beyond utility, beyond the pleasure of recognizing ourselves in the past or meeting fascinating strangers there, the study of history, when widespread in a community or among a people, confers on them a power of which Webb was acutely aware and which he tried to describe for his students and readers. His words in that same preface to the Texas county histories put it most movingly: "Books accumulate in the community, knowledge spreads about the community, and the people come to feel that they have a culture and a civilization of their own and not something borrowed or brought in for a summer trip. . . . We can never have real education, or a self-perpetuating culture, until we get beyond the description and the describer to the things described."[36]

He meant, of course, that knowing history endows everything we see and touch with additional meanings—not a single overarching one, but a multitude of associations as real as the object or the scene itself. Life is made thicker, richer, of weightier import because other beings than ourselves—yet kindred—have passed where we walk. Through our knowledge of their history, which is as well *our* history, what they left, where they trod, what they willed cease to be abstractions or even symbols; they become parts of the common memory, enshrined in the common language; and thereby those beings and their deeds are living still.

NOTES

1. That colleague is Professor Henry F. Graff of the Columbia University History Department.

2. Walter Prescott Webb, *An Honest Preface and Other Essays, with an Appreciative Introduction by Joe B. Frantz*, (Boston, 1959), 201ff.

3. Ibid., 202, 203.

4. Ibid., 198, 205.

5. Ibid., 207.

6. Ibid., 104.

7. Ibid., 106, 205.

8. Ibid., 205.

9. Ibid., 198, 206, 107.

10. Turner and Webb in their own day might have made themselves familiar with the works of the climatologist and interpreter of civilizations, Ellsworth Huntington, which appeared beginning in 1910.

11. In Montesquieu, *L'Esprit des Lois* (mistranslated as "Spirit" when it should be "Meaning"), see Bk. 19, where the several causes are summarized.

12. Webb, *Honest Preface*, 108.

13. Concurrently in the United States, James Harvey Robinson and others advocated and practiced "the New History," which tended to be the history of "great ideas" and the mass movements they generated. It was not as sociological as the French prototype but equally faceless.

14. Webb, *Honest Preface*, 198.

15. Quoted in G. R. Elton, *The Practice of History* (New York, 1967), 127.

16. For a vivid account of the state of fact and feeling in historiography, see Frederic Harrison, "The History Schools, an Oxford Dialogue," (1893) in *The Meaning of History* (London, 1907).

17. These titles are taken from a recent (Spring, 1984) university press catalogue. A similar list could be drawn from *any* university press catalogue. The new journals carry out the theme: *The Journal of the History of Childhood, The Journal of Peasant History*, and so on. Collections of essays follow suit: *The History of Urban France; Horses in European Economic History, a Preliminary Canter*, etc.

18. Webb, *Honest Preface*, 74.

19. Estes Kefauver, *Crime in America* (New York, 1951).

20. See "The Historical Seminar: Its Outer Shell and Its Inner Spirit" in Webb, *Honest Preface*, 143–70, and also 136–39, 177–78.

21. Ibid., 204.

22. Ibid., 107.

23. Ibid., 132–35.

24. Ibid., 151.

25. Theodore Zeldin, *France: 1848–1945*, 2 vols. (Oxford, 1973), 1: 2–3.

26. Ibid., 1:22.

27. Ibid., 1:87.

28. Ibid., 1:287.

29. Ibid., 1:286.

30. J. H. Plumb, *Encounter* 40 (April, 1973): 64.

31 Jonathan Israel, London *Times Literary Supplement*, Jan. 21, 1983, 63.

32. A plea for a "return to chronology" was made by the French Minister of Education at a conference on teaching history held at the university of Montpellier in January, 1984. This lone voice amid the promoters of the "social problem approach" was reported with approval in a number of French newspapers, notably *Le Figaro* for January 23, 1984.

33. "A Simple Discipline—the Teaching of History," unpublished paper delivered at Princeton University Bicentennial Conference, February 20, 1947, 5.

34. Walter Shapiro, *The Washington Monthly*, March, 1981, 48.

35. *Seminar Reports* (Columbia University) 2, January 27, 1975, 3.

36. Webb, *Honest Preface*, 70, 71.

ELLIOTT WEST

Cowboys and Indians and Artists and Liars and Schoolmarms and Tom Mix: New Ways to Teach the American West

UNLIKE some academics, Walter Prescott Webb could never see the boundary between the worlds of teacher and scholar. The career that would make him one of the nation's most famous historians began in the high schools of Beeville and Cuero. His first professional recognition came in 1916 with an article on classroom technique, and forty years later, after *The Great Plains* and *The Great Frontier* had brought him huzzahs from the scholarly community, he devoted his presidential address before the Mississippi Valley Historical Association to the glories of the seminar. In him, the original and persuasive researcher and writer lived easily with the patient, popular teacher.[1]

It follows that Webb would be pleased by what is happening in what he once called his "plebian field of Western America."[2] During the past twenty years, historians have brought fresh insights and methodologies to the study of western history. There is good evidence today that this new scholarship has started to percolate from the library stacks into undergraduate classrooms, and the results have been interesting.

One indication of this change is found in a survey I conducted recently among 122 historians of the American West. This essay will not focus on the results of that survey, but they can provide some observations and an occasional point of reference. The survey, for instance, shows clearly that teachers are ranging far beyond the traditional topics of explorers, iron horses, and sodbusters to bring in a score of subjects all but ignored a generation ago. To some, this might seem like the cavalry officer, described in a student's exam, who "jumped on his horse and rode off in all directions." But in fact there is a pattern. Teachers have come to approach the history of the West from three basic perspectives. Each of these approaches in turn is evolving and expanding as it absorbs the new western scholarship. Together these changes reveal a remarkable flowering in the teaching of courses that students, with a blend of affection and condescension, are fond of calling "Cowboys and Indians."

The first of these three approaches is the most traditional. Western history is taught as "westward expansion," and within this approach a vigorous reconstruction is underway. Yet this revision by no means involves a rejection of the original inspiration for this way of teaching—the frontier thesis of Frederick Jackson Turner. In fact, almost precisely half of those surveyed are using the Turner thesis as the "primary interpretive focus" of their courses, and most of the rest are giving it a prominent place in their lectures. Now in its tenth decade, the bloody and battered frontier thesis has held up remarkably well. Certainly it has never retired from the classroom.

The reasons for Turner's continuing appeal are clear enough. The story of westward expansion is one of the great dramas of American history, and one whose appeal is not limited to persons living west of the Mississippi. At some point the frontier moved through every part of our country, and Turner found in this process a sweeping explanation for what has made Americans different from everyone else. This approach has something to say to students from Boston and Tucson, Boise and Youngstown. It raises provocative questions about the influence of culture and environment.[3] And finally, perhaps because it touches on certain deep-seated myths, students seem to find it quite persuasive. "It is almost impossible in the classroom to defeat Turner one-on-one," a teacher admitted. In no other field has the thinking of one person held on so stubbornly for so long.

On the other hand, as the survey clearly shows, just about everyone teaching western history today agrees that for all its value, the traditional Turnerian approach leaves out much that happened. Increasingly, teachers are trying to fill in the story. For an obvious case in point, a reader need only take a close look at the archetypal figures of Turner's frontier procession. The trappers and hunters and farmers are intrepid, innovative, fiercely nationalistic, violent by nature—and all men. There is not a petticoat in the lot.

Among the roughly two thousand pages of Turner's published works, he included one paragraph that focused on the role of women on the frontier, and until recently other historians have not done much better. When seen at all, women typically appear as crudely drawn stereotypes, particularly as rather passive helpmates of pioneer men, largely unable to cope by themselves with the new conditions of the frontier.[4]

But this sexual bias, at least in its crudest form, now seems to be fast disappearing from the classroom. Of the teachers surveyed, more than six out of ten devoted a full lecture or more specifically to women in the West. Only 6 percent had no formal presentation on women. It is equally interesting that 35 percent of those who include women in their lectures have done so only during the past five years. If this survey is any indication, things are changing quickly. This shift, furthermore, surely reflects recent historiographical trends, for instructors can now take advantage of a rapidly growing list of studies that are changing and broadening the historical perception of women in the West.

These works show, for example, that a surprising number of frontier women lived—and often prospered—on their own. In northeastern Colorado nearly one homestead in five was worked by a single woman. On the mining frontier, as many as a fourth of all family households were headed by mothers without husbands, and though most of these single mothers worked in domestic tasks, some were successful businesswomen who ran hotels and restaurants, grubstaked prospectors, and occasionally managed mining properties. Another study shows that Arizona widows were a shrewd lot, expanding their inheritances at a rate faster than the local economy, and yet another, set far to the north in Helena, Montana, reveals that a third of the prostitutes in 1870 were "Capitalists with Rooms," who controlled money and property worth, on the average, a thousand dollars more than the typical man who bought their favors.[5]

Nonetheless, most frontier women lived and worked with husbands as part of family households, and the picture of these frontierswomen is changing, too. Some scholars have begun to analyze the sexual division of labor in the West. Rather than simply allowing men to get on with the "real" work of the frontier, the rigorous and extraordinarily diverse labors of wives and mothers contributed to the family economy at least as much as the fathers' work.[6] Yet in directing their own lives and those of their children, these women often enjoyed nothing close to equality. By concentrating on this "political economy of sex," writers have opened the way to a fuller understanding of women's economic contributions as well as of power relationships within the family. With such work has come a growing curiosity about women's emotional responses to life on the frontier. Scores of diaries, letters and other private writings, largely ignored until lately, finally are being read and studied, and though writers are coming away from these documents with varying conclusions, teachers today are able to discuss with their students some fascinating questions about the inner world of Western women.[7]

The impact of women on frontier life and society, moreover, was never confined to the home. Playing upon their image as protectors of children and symbols of propriety, women helped shape the social tone and even the urban landscape of their communities through temperance crusades and promotion of churches and schools.[8] Frontier prostitutes played an ironic role in this: by standing out as an outrageous and highly visible foil to respectable womanhood, a recent book observes, these soiled doves indirectly reinforced the standards of the Victorian home in emerging frontier towns. Still another study suggests that in the latter stages of the mining frontier, miners' wives took an active part in the development of unions and their struggle for recognition.[9]

In fact, western women's studies have led into many other unexpected areas. They have thrown new light on what happened when the advancing frontier came into contact with peoples already on the land. No figure symbolizes the self-reliant male frontiersman more than the mountain man, for instance, but recent research by Sylvia Van Kirk and others demonstrates the critical role played in the fur trade by Indian wives of trappers and traders. The irony, of course, is that these women helped clear the way for the coming European institutions so destructive to their own cultures.[10] Indeed, studies of intermarriage, family, and households elsewhere in the West—Texas, New Mexico, and California, among other places—have provided a fresh perspective on the ways Anglo-American culture first mingled with and finally dominated once flourishing Hispanic and Indian peoples.[11]

I have paused this long in women's history to show how new research in this one area is contributing to a fundamental change in the older picture of the frontier experience. Most teachers surely would agree that they should never again talk about westward expansion strictly in the male gender. More than that, however, this recent scholarship calls for a redefinition of the entire pioneering process, a de-emphasis of the solitary male frontiersman, for example, and a focus instead on the family as a much more significant force in westward expansion.

A half dozen other areas of new research make much the same point. Two in particular are finding their way into the classroom. First, there is a growing appreciation for the many non-Anglo ethnic groups who took part in westward expansion. Turner claimed that the magical frontier process acted upon everyone who came there, turning them into a new type—the American. Where the frontiersman came from was far less important than what happened to him after he arrived. As a result, western historians have neglected a fundamental fact: the frontier was the most ethnically diverse region of American life in the late nineteenth and early twentieth centuries. In many mining towns more than half of all adults had been born abroad; in Shoshone County, Idaho, in 1870, for instance, a stunning 87 percent of the population was foreign-born. Thirty years later the census bureau reported that nearly eight out of ten persons living on the broad plains of North Dakota were immigrants or the children of immigrants. No state or territory in American history has ever matched that figure.[12]

Nor did these pioneers come from only a few nations with similar cultures. They hailed from England, Ireland, China, and the Azores. There were Cornishmen, Frenchmen, Italians, Germans, Mexicans, Belgians, Russians, Finns, Czechs, Poles, Scots, Turks, West Indians, and Hawaiians. In the promised land they were not quickly made over. How they responded to the frontier depended in part on their cultural origins, and teachers can now call upon an expanding body of work, both overviews of western ethnic history and many specialized studies, to understand this process better.[13]

There is even an article on Serbs in Arizona and an entire book on Yugoslavs in Nevada.[14]

Likewise, Turner's emphasis on the pioneer farmer has tended to obscure the fact that towns and cities always have played crucial roles in the history of the frontier, particularly beyond the Mississippi. Since around 1850, when the far West emerged in the census as a distinct region, it has been second only to the Northeast as the most urbanized part of the country. In 1970 it officially became number one. So it makes sense for teachers to pay more attention to the promotion and patterns of growth of western urban centers—mining and cattle towns, markets, logging camps, and ports on rivers and on the Pacific. From these places much can be learned about the economic, social, and cultural developments that came with westward expansion.[15]

In other areas—the history of labor and unionization, religion, science, technology, and business, for instance—recent research apparently is persuading instructors to revise drastically some older ways of looking at the American frontier. The cumulative effect has been a broadening of the grand story associated with Turner's name.

Even after these revisions, the Turner thesis has some inherent limitations. It asks us to focus on the changes born from three centuries of adaptation as those European-American pioneers marched, more or less westward, across the continent. Anything not fitting into this framework is considered unimportant. Many teachers find this far too confining. "[It] feels like a straightjacket, and I cannot comfortably teach with it on," as one instructor explained. For many students, there is another problem. The frontier experience has been over for at least three generations now, and each new crop of freshmen lives a bit farther from it. The shaping influence that Turner described has less direct meaning to our lives with each year that passes, and to many students in search of a subject, that seems to make western history guilty of that most unforgivable of sins—irrelevance.

However, there is a second approach to the teaching of western history which offers the possibility of more effectively engaging student interest. Instead of being studied as a frontier, western history can be told as the story of a geographically and historically distinct region. This approach has proved increasingly popular, particularly among teachers in the West itself. One of these, John E. Sunder of the University of Texas at Austin, covers four hundred years of western history from the plains to the Pacific and the borderlands to the Arctic, in a flexible format that includes "Comparative History . . . , Empire History, Colonial History and Cultural History." Others, like Richard M. Brown of the University of Oregon, draw inspiration from the new intellectual respectability that such works as Emmanuel Wallerstein's *Modern World System* have given to the study of regionalism. Finally, an upsurge in off-campus interest in local history has brought students flocking to classes that tell the history of their state and the country around it. These classes, in fact, often draw better than ones in traditional western history. When the late K. Ross Toole taught an upper-level course in Montana history at the University of Montana in 1980–81, his combined enrollment in two terms totaled an astounding 1,735.

Those who teach about the West as a region begin with the land itself. Anyone who has traveled there, of course, recognizes that there are many Wests—the high and low plains, the Rockies, the Southwestern borderlands, the Great Basin or Mormon Corridor, the plateaus, and the Pacific slope. But taken as a whole, the West does have a certain unity within its diversity. It is an uncommon land, as the journalist Samuel Bowles noted when he toured it in 1869. "The eastern half of America," he wrote, "offers no suggestion of its western half."[16] Writers before and since Bowles have scrambled to find words to describe the country to outsiders. The novelist Mary Austin probably came closest with her four choices: God, death, beauty, madness. Certainly it is a land of extremes. Westerners are addicted to puffing out their chests and pointing out that among the forty-eight contiguous states, the seventeen farthest to the west have the hottest and coldest spots, the highest and lowest, the wettest and driest. In them are America's deepest lake, its youngest mountains, and its oldest trees.

In terms of the West's human history, three geographic characteristics stand out. The West contains enormously rich resources: not only timber and fertile soil, but also precious and non-precious metals, petroleum, and natural gas in far greater quantities than in the East. Second, the West's great size, along with the nature of its resources, has made it a region of cities—"urban oases"—surrounded by great yawning spaces.[17] Finally, most of the West is arid or semi-arid. Much of the Pacific coast and parts of the mountains are well watered, but the rest generally gets less than twenty inches of rain a year, and some sections less than two. Those teaching the West as a region concentrate upon the continuing interplay between this landscape and two other elements—the customs and traditions brought into the land, and the many changing influences from the world outside.

Turner himself came to believe that a regional approach offered many insights into the social, political, and economic history of the West and the United States, and he spent much of his later career developing his "sectional thesis."[18] But the man most associated with the study of the West as a region is the one who inspired these lectures, Walter Prescott Webb. Webb was interested in the frontier experience, but he argued that the force of the western environment would be felt not just during that special historical moment but as long as people lived there. In his masterwork, Webb considered *The Great Plains* the heart of the West, "a geographic unity whose influences have been so powerful as to put a characteristic mark upon everything that survives within its borders." His attention roamed far beyond Turner's frontiersmen. Into the picture came Hispanics and Indians, even prairie dogs and antelopes. It was a grander story of how "this land . . . has from the beginning worked its inexorable effect upon nature's children."[19]

This approach offers teachers some important advantages. Much more comfortably than Turner's frontier thesis, for example, it allows a full appreciation of the many cultures that have flourished in the West. Hispanics appeared there more than two hundred years before the Anglo- and Euro-American invaders from the east, and the American Indians at least twenty thousand years before that. These peoples arrived with vastly different expectations and different loads of cultural baggage. From the Turnerian point of view, however, they are worth studying not so much in their own right but simply because they stood in the way of the frontier. They were barriers that had meaning mainly in relation to those who eventually dominated them.

Using Webb's approach, each of these groups, and many more,

can fill a separate chapter in an old drama of a unique land. Writers have recently begun to expand upon this second approach to western history. The historical geographer Donald W. Meinig has focused upon the Southwest and the Columbian plain to show the interaction of different cultural groups with the changing environment. David J. Weber, Terry Jordan, Richard V. Francaviglia, and Richard White have taken as their subjects Mexicans, Germans, Mormons, Pawnees, and Navajos. They have written from the point of view of each of these peoples, examining the continuing dynamic relationship between these groups, their setting, and those who have influenced them. The results have given us original and provocative insights into the western experience.[20] Teachers who take advantage of this kind of scholarship can portray the history of the West not just as a progression of one pioneer type toward the Pacific, but rather as a series of changing cultural systems, each acting upon and feeling the impact of others—Pueblos and Navajos, Navajos and Hispanics, Hispanics and Anglos, Mormons, Californios, Chinese, and Basques.[21]

There is another important consequence that flows from teaching the West as regional history. Anyone who does so will be much more likely to take the story into the twentieth century. After all, though the frontier is gone, the West remains. When Turner delivered his invitation to his fellow historians in 1893, about ninety years had passed since Lewis and Clark ascended the Missouri and set in motion the juggernaut of far western expansion. It now has been ninety years since Turner spoke, yet until recently specialists in western history, mesmerized by the frontier thesis, have paid scant attention to most of what has happened in the region since then. For most students, the West of the twentieth century remains a vast unexplored territory.[22] That is a pity, because the history of the modern West has great potential appeal in the classroom. Walter Webb knew that better than most, and some of that appeal can be demonstrated by looking at what he had to say about the recent West and updating it a bit.

Webb wrote two controversial pieces about the West and its future. The first, in 1937, was *Divided We Stand*.[23] In it Webb argued that the West—and the South—lived in economic bondage to the Northeast. The West, he wrote, contained many of the country's most important natural resources, but by a variety of yardsticks of wealth and power—savings deposits, ownership of stocks and bonds, life insurance policies, and even advertisers in the *Saturday Evening Post*—the Northeast, with only 5 to 10 percent of the nation's resources, controlled 80 to 90 percent of its wealth. Webb was raising again the bitter charges of the Populists and, more recently, the arguments of *Harper's* editor Bernard DeVoto, who had called the West a "Plundered Province" in an article four years before Webb's book. Americans, they all said, lived under a feudal system, and westerners and southerners were the serfs.

Twenty years later, Webb himself published an article in *Harper's*, titled "The American West, Perpetual Mirage."[24] Here he argued that much of the West, from the Missouri River to California and from Oklahoma to Canada, is best thought of as a desert. The region's sprawling interior has vast riches in minerals, oil and gas, and timber, but it lacks the vital, all-important element of water. In the long run, this country could never support a large population, Webb wrote, and so it could never enjoy a full flowering of cultural life. He was saying again that the land always will put its mark on everything that survives upon it. Despite its special mystique, the West would forever remain a land of unalterable deficiencies.

These two pieces provoked regional attacks against the Texas historian, but anyone who looks beyond his critics' injured pride and their gas and bunkum will quickly see that Webb was touching on two questions of exceptional importance. Is there a sectional imbalance in this country that leads, among other things, to exploitation of the West by outside economic interests? And what limits, if any, does the western environment place on the people who live there?

Today these two questions are even more interesting and pressing than when Webb raised them, mainly because of the most important development in the modern West—the astonishing growth of its population. The state with the most dizzying growth has been California. Between 1900 and 1970 its population increased by more than nineteen million, a figure that roughly equals all the persons who emigrated to the United States during the entire nineteenth century. Beyond California, all the West has grown, especially since World War II. In 1947, about one out of nine Amer-

icans lived in the western states; today about one in five does. Of
the seventeen westernmost states, only four—North and South Dakota, Kansas, and Nebraska—did not grow faster than the national
average from 1970 to 1980. Of the twelve fastest growing states in
the country, eleven are in the West, and there is little indication
that this will change anytime soon. One recent study measured the
regional preferences of those Americans wishing to move to another part of the country. In this sectional popularity poll, the
mountain states and the Southwest ran away from the pack; the
Pacific coast was second, followed by the South, while the Northeast and the Ohio valley ran last.[25]

With this flood of population has come a growth in the western
economy, but even more important have been certain changes
within the region's economic structure. The West traditionally has
depended heavily upon only two sectors of the economy—agriculture and mining, especially the former. With most of their eggs in
two baskets, some observers say, westerners have been particularly
vulnerable to control and manipulation from outside the region.[26]

Since the end of World War II, however, the western economy
has undergone a remarkable diversification. Three developments
have had a special impact. Western tourism and entertainment
have boomed as vacationers have discovered the climatic comforts
and scenic marvels of that unique land. As one measure of this,
more than fifteen thousand new motels and hotels sprang up along
western highways between 1945 and 1960. Second, there has been
a prodigious expansion of manufacturing; statistically speaking, this
has been the most rapidly growing sector. Some of this growth has
come in traditional heavy industries, such as steel plants in Colorado and Utah, but more significant have been high-tech industries
spawned by the technological revolution of the last generation; in
1961, for instance, one out of every five electronics workers in the
country lived in California. Finally, the federal government has
showered the West with billions of dollars in defense contracts. It
may be debated whether in the long run this money is better com-
pared to manna from heaven or acid rain, but it is undeniable that
in the short term defense spending his contributed mightily to
western prosperity.[27]

As a result, the West has moved rapidly away from its reliance on farming and mining. Those two industries have grown as well, but not nearly as much as the others just mentioned. Equally interesting, these newly emerging industries, all of them likely to continue to grow in the future, are expanding much faster than in other parts of the country, especially the Northeast. Between 1947 and 1977, nonagricultural employment in the northeastern states grew by about 35 percent, while in the West the pace was 172 percent, well ahead of even the region's prodigious population growth. In defense spending, California has profited most of all; in 1961, twenty-four cents out of every dollar spent on defense went to that one state. But other western states have hardly been ignored. The federal government in 1976 contributed $32 per person in defense salaries in New York, about $58 in Massachusetts, and $85 in New Jersey. The average in Montana was $132, $275 in Colorado, and $306 in Utah.[28]

Politically the turn-of-the-century West, as the youngest and most sparsely populated part of the country, found it difficult to make itself heard in Washington, D.C. The growth in population, however, has changed all that. Consider the shift in political power from Northeast to West as reflected in the House of Representatives. In 1900 the ten states of the Northeast elected 28 percent of the House membership, the West only 15 percent. In 1940 the Northeast held steady at 28 percent, while the West had edged up to 21, but then the geopolitical tide really began to turn. Today the situation of 1940 has been reversed. The West elects 28 percent, the Northeast 22. Given the present trends of our migratory people, the gap in the House will surely widen much more by the next century. Changes in the electoral votes in each section have followed precisely this same pattern.[29]

Some results of this westward tilt are obvious even to casual observers. We live with a president from California and a vice-president from Texas, and in fact of the seven presidents elected since World War II, five have been from west of the Mississippi. With its recent Republican blooming, the Senate has important committees chaired by Mark Hatfield, John Tower, Robert Dole, Jake Garn, Orrin Hatch, and James McClure—westerners, all of them—while the Democratic House kept as its majority leader Jim Wright of Texas.[30]

Some surely will argue that these changes have not necessarily ended the sectional exploitation that Webb described. Colonialism is admittedly difficult to measure. More representatives do not always mean better representation, and economic figures are notoriously slippery. Some critics would add that to protect themselves westerners must also develop a sense of regional unity and purpose, but political conservatism, ingrained individualism, and most of all distrust and jealousy among the states have so far frustrated moves in that direction.[31] Nevertheless, the situation Webb described is changing dramatically. Looking at what has been happening, the author of *Divided We Stand* might well conclude that the West is at last breaking free of its vassalage to the Northeast.

But, he would quickly add, there is a catch. The most spectacular growth has come deep in the heart of the western desert—in southern California, Colorado, Arizona, New Mexico, Nevada, and Wyoming. And the evidence is overwhelming that the available water simply cannot support those living in these places now, much less the millions who seem determined to move there. The local water supply of Denver can comfortably provide for only about 20 percent of its present population, and San Diego's, about 13 percent. As developers have reached outward for what they need, they naturally have begun to fight for what little there is, most bitterly in the struggle between Arizona and southern California for control of the Colorado River.[32] Compounding the problem of too many thirsty people are two other demands. Some of the manufacturing that has boosted the region's economy demands huge amounts of its most precious commodity, and agriculture, always a mainstay in the West's economic well being, has come to rely to an extraordinary degree upon irrigation. Of every hundred gallons of water used daily in the United States, eighty-three run onto irrigated fields, much of it in the arid lands beyond the ninety-eighth meridian. The vast aquifers feeding the pumps there are being used up at an alarming rate. Report after report on water in the West has come to the same glum conclusion Webb did twenty-five years ago: there just is not enough.[33]

So in the West of 1984, two developments seem set on a collision course. The very changes that are bringing westerners prosperity may well be drawing them into an ecological disaster. It is a fascinating contradiction, and it shows that Webb still has a lot to say to us. He probably would add that if we think of the West not just as a frontier but also as a distinctive region, these and many other issues would come into focus. To what extent has the influx of new people and the impact of the mass media eroded the West's distinctive cultural traits? How has the experimentation in life-styles so characteristic of California and other areas infected the world outside the region's borders? Has the West been truly inno-vative, reshaping our institutions, or as Earl Pomeroy and others have suggested, has it been a conservative force in American soci-ety?[34] For the student looking for subjects that speak immediately to his world, the recent history of the West is as pertinent a course as he can find.

But this second approach to the study of western history also has its problems. For all its significance to the American scene, Webb's way still teaches about only one region of the country. It can never offer what Turner did—thoughts about the formation of a collective American character and a story that touches all parts of the nation. If Turner leaves us stranded in the past, Webb confines us to one part of the land. The limits of the two are basic—time and space.

Fortunately, there is a third perspective. This approach, used by a growing minority of teachers, considers the West not in the traditional sense of history at all. Instead it deals with its mythic dimension—that is, not what in fact happened but what people have believed and imagined about the western experience.

Far more than the other two, this way of teaching inspires heated, even impassioned opposition from those who see it as an attempt to lend respectability to the study of fads and foolishness. The "special topics" courses that have blossomed at many schools have drawn particularly heavy fire. One such course considers "John Wayne: An American Hero in Myth and Legend." In another, enrollees study Western "B" movies, including "Arizona Terror" (1931), "Public Cowboy No. 1" (1937), and "Wild Horse Rustlers" (1943), a Bob Livingston cliff-hanger in which Nazis in Stetsons try to bushwhack the U.S. cavalry. There are those who see this as pandering to students in a search for higher enrollments. "We offer courses in public history, rock and roll music, and the comics, . . ." wrote one critic. "What has happened?"

But courses like these are only the hem of the garment—amusing exercises that entice the student to study rich, complex themes in American culture. They also emphasize an important point: for good or ill, it is the myth more than the reality that attracts many who choose classes in western history. Asked to explain the appeal of their subject, those surveyed answered again and again that students come through their doors looking for "adventure," "color," "romance," and "stereotypical images of cowboys and Indians." Many instructors take advantage of what one called this "perversion of reality" by contrasting, as starkly as possible, what students think happened with what actually did.

The possibilities, however, go far beyond that. The western myth deserves attention for four reasons. It motivated the pioneers themselves, and so it helps explain the frontier's rapid expansion. From it, furthermore, has come a profusion of enduring literary and artistic themes. The myth also opens a window into the popular mind, and by studying it over time, one can trace changes in the ways Americans have thought about themselves. Finally, the values associated with the western myth continue to shape our styles of living and the ways we respond to the world around us.

Recent scholarly interest in the western myth can be traced to the publication in 1950 of Henry Nash Smith's *Virgin Land: The American West as Symbol and Myth*.[35] Writers since then have built upon the idea that what Americans have believed about the West comes as close as anything ever has to a national mythology expressing a distinctive American set of values, fears, biases, and aspirations. Through this myth Americans have announced to the world who they are and how they have come to be that way. This myth emerged during the first few generations after the American Revolution. Unlike Europeans, we had no long history to draw upon, so instead we made a virtue of the fact that we had no past. We were a fresh beginning. The American was a New-World Adam, reborn out of his struggles with the abundant, threatening wilderness. This new American hero combined an innocence and an instinctive sense of justice with strength, self-reliance, and a free-roaming individualism.

In this way our national myth and sense of uniqueness was married to westward expansion. We distorted and rearranged this history and made larger-than-life figures of the men who lived there. Boone was the first, and following him were an army of others from Custer to Billy the Kid. Joining them were fully fictional characters. Among the most enduring was the earliest—James Fenimore Cooper's Leatherstocking—but there were scores of others. Some have suggested that with so little human history to draw from, Americans made heroes of the land itself. Spain has the Cid; we have the Grand Canyon.[36]

This American myth quickly grabbed the attention of Europeans, both the mass reading public and the intellectual elite. Boone showed up in Byron's *Don Juan*. In *The Cossacks*, Tolstoy stole from Cooper's plots. Dumas entitled one of his stories *Les Mohicans de Paris*, and in 1828 the towering genius of his age, Goethe, considered writing a western novel. Historians now are beginning to trace how western images have shaped the European perception of the United States and how the myth may have influenced intellectual currents on the continent. It is a continuing story; the western myth remains one of the most reliable American exports.[37]

It has flourished most vigorously, of course, in its native soil. Early in the twentieth century, the myth left for good the forests of Leatherstocking and moved into the Far West, where the majestic mountains, rolling plains, and desert vistas provided the perfect backdrop for its exaggerated heroics. The cowboy quickly emerged as the quintessential American hero. As the frontier came to a close, the myth actually gathered strength, and like a great oak it spread outward from its original source, each branch sending out others that grew and divided again and again.

Scholars of the modern myth have looked most intently at its place in popular and mass culture, and they have paid closest attention to film and television.[38] In a way that is a pity, because the recent decline of horse operas on the silver screen and the picture tube has given the impression that the Western is on the wane. But elsewhere it is as vigorous as ever. Mass-market western novels, for instance, continue to sell at a phenomenal pace. The acknowledged king, and one of the four best-selling authors alive, is Louis L'Amour, whose eighty-four books have sold more than 130 million copies. Today the public is buying them at a rate of five hundred thousand a month. In the world of advertising, the appeal of the western motif goes far beyond the famous Marlboro man. Even in *New Yorker, Cosmopolitan*, and other periodicals catering mainly to eastern readers, slick images full of chaps and Winchesters lend an aura of integrity, adventure, romance, and virility to products ranging from coffee and eyeblush to cologne and dish antennas. Elsewhere the "urban cowboy" craze is settling down, and the republic no longer trembles from the bucking of thousands of mechanical bulls, but the popularity of country and western music continues unabated. Though the contents of the lyrics increasingly focus on domestic tensions, they do so with a vernacular and style unmistakably part of the mythic frontier tradition. Less obvious is the way the myth has shaped rock and roll. There the theme of the individual's westward quest for freedom and hedonistic pleasures has found fertile ground, whether in the innocence of the Beach Boys, the irony of the Eagles, or the macho exuberance of "that little ole band from Texas," Z Z Top.[39]

The Western myth has played a prominent role in another area of mass culture—politics. After Jackson, William Henry Harrison, and Lincoln first exploited it, the myth fell into disuse for a while, only to blossom again in the career of Theodore Roosevelt. Politicians since him have used effectively two techniques pioneered by that "cowboy president." Lyndon Johnson, Barry Goldwater, and Ronald Reagan have clothed themselves in the imagery of the western hero, thereby assuring voters that they are their own men, honest, straightforward, and steady in a crisis. These and others, including the impeccably eastern John F. Kennedy, have sought to sell their programs by appealing to the public's identification of the best of our national character with the frontier experience, no matter how farfetched the comparison may be. So Kennedy called his reforms for an urban, industrialized society the "new frontier," and Richard M. Nixon once urged Americans to leave Vietnam only "as a cowboy, with guns blazing, backing out of a saloon."[40]

In the realm of high culture, artists have forsaken the simple formulas used so effectively by politicians, advertising men, and pulp novelists, but they still have found in the West a metaphor for the American experience and its paradoxes. Through the work of Twain, Whitman, Garland, Cather, Hemingway, Steinbeck, and even Melville and Fitzgerald can be found the theme of the new land's promise and cruelty and its part in shaping a unique national spirit. New studies like John R. Milton's *The Novel of the American West* go beyond these masters to treat seriously the likes of Vardis Fisher, Frederick Manfred, Harvey Fergusson, Wallace Stegner, A. B. Guthrie, Jr., and other writers dismissed as regionalists by earlier critics. Ken Kesey, Larry McMurtry, and a younger generation of novelists have continued the tradition. In poetry, a reader need only turn to Joaquin Miller, Theodore Roethke, Robinson Jeffers, and Gary Snyder, and in contemporary drama to Arthur Kopit, Preston Jones, and Sam Shepard.[41]

Anyone interested in teaching the West as myth, then, can choose from a smorgasbord of subjects and sources, and shelves of new books and articles can be expected in this field during the next few years. Through this approach a teacher can raise intriguing questions. How much does this recurring dream of the West affect our individual and collective decisions? Does it still shape the image we present to the rest of the world, as Richard Nixon recently suggested when he urged President Reagan to meet with Soviet leaders to convince them he is not a "reckless cowboy"? Does our fascination with the myth reveal a continuing tension in the American spirit between the two basic frontier impulses, the need to be free and the need to be rich?

Best of all, it is the myth that brings together the ways of teaching the West suggested by Turner and Webb, and it overcomes in part their limitations of time and space. The West of the imagination was born of Turner's frontier, and along the way it has found its home beyond the Big River in that improbable country Webb described so brilliantly. The myth celebrates both. Through it, a distant land and a vanished time continue to speak to most of us in a thousand telling ways.

Webb would have understood. After all, he was acquainted early in his life with each of these perspectives. As a child of four he migrated with his family, in the classic pioneer pattern, from the cotton fields of Panola County to a hardscrabble farm near Ranger in West Texas. There he was thrust against the new land and felt the power of that "open, arid country which stretched north and west farther than a boy could imagine." And on this fringe of the Great Plains he listened to the buffalo hunters, boomers, and cowboys whose tales of the near past was the stuff of the myth already feeding a hungry public.[42]

Today, twenty years after Webb's untimely passing, an expanding body of new work is broadening our understanding of the frontier, of western regional studies, and of the national vision that embraces it all. The teacher's challenge is to tell about western history with a decent respect for all these points of view, remaining faithful to the facts but also to the fancy that has nurtured the story and knit together its many parts. It is the tension among these elements that gives the field its special vitality. Forty years ago T. K. Whipple described our bond to those who were drawn to the frontier. "What they dreamed, we live; what they lived, we dream," he wrote. "That is why our Western story still holds us, however ineptly it is told."[43]

The message for the classrooms is clear: it is time to tell it better.

NOTES

    1. Walter Rundell, Jr., "Webb the Schoolteacher," in Kenneth R. Philp and Elliott West, eds., *Essays on Walter Prescott Webb* (Austin: University of Texas Press, 1976), 95–123; Walter Prescott Webb, "The Historical Seminar: Its Outer Shell and Its Inner Spirit," in *An Honest Preface and Other Essays* (Boston: Houghton Mifflin Co., 1959), 143–70.

    2. Walter Prescott Webb, "History as High Adventure," in *Honest Preface*, 196.

    3. More probably has been written on Turner than on any other American historian. The student should begin with Ray Allen Billington, *Frederick Jackson Turner: Historian, Scholar, Teacher* (New York: Oxford University Press, 1973) and his *America's Frontier Heritage* (New York: Holt Rinehart and Winston, 1966). For recent examples of different opinions and approaches to the Turner thesis, see Jackson K. Putnam, "The Turner Thesis and the Westward Movement: A Reappraisal," *Western Historical Quarterly* 7 (October, 1976): 377–404; Margaret Walsh, *The American Frontier Revisited* (Atlantic Highlands, New Jersey: Humanities Press, 1981); Harry N. Scheiber, "Turner's Legacy and the Search for a Reorientation of Western History: A Review Essay," *New Mexico Historical Review* 44 (July, 1969):

231–48; Jerome O. Steffan, "Some Observations on the Turner Thesis: A Polemic," *Papers in Anthropology* 14 (Spring, 1973): 32–40; Jim Potter, "Some British Reflections on Turner and the Frontier," *Wisconsin Magazine of History* 53 (Winter, 1969–70): 98–107.

4. The mention of women in Turner's work is from Richard Jensen, "On Modernizing Frederick Jackson Turner," *Western Historical Quarterly* 11 (July, 1980): 307–22. On stereotypes of frontier women, see Beverly J. Stoeltje, "'A Helpmate for Man Indeed': The Image of the Frontier Woman," *Journal of American Folklore* 88 (January–March, 1975): 25–41. A reader interested in the history of women in the West should begin with two recent works, Sandra L. Myres, *Westering Women and the Frontier Experience, 1800–1915* (Albuquerque: University of New Mexico Press, 1982) and Julie Roy Jeffrey, *Frontier Women: The Trans-Mississippi West, 1840–1880* (New York: Hill and Wang, 1979), as well as historiographical essays, Joan M. Jensen and Darlis A. Miller, "The Gentle Tamers Revisited: New Approaches to the History of Women in the American West," *Pacific Historical Review* 49 (May, 1980): 173–213; Paula A. Treckel, "An Historiographical Essay: Women on the American Frontier," *Old Northwest* 1 (December, 1975): 391–403; and Sandra L. Myres, "Women in the West," in Michael P. Malone, ed., *Historians and the American West* (Lincoln: University of Nebraska Press, 1983), 369–86.

5. Sheryll Patterson-Black, "Women Homesteaders on the Great Plains Frontier," *Frontiers* 1 (Spring, 1976): 67–88; Elliott West, "Women of the Rocky Mountain West," in Duane A. Smith, ed., *A Taste of the West: Essays in Honor of Robert G. Athearn* (Boulder: Pruett Press, 1983), 148–73; Margaret S. Woyski, "Women and Mining in the Old West," *Journal of the West* 20 (April, 1981): 38–47; Laurie Alberts, "Petticoats and Pickaxes," *Alaska Journal* 7 (Summer, 1977): 146–59; Myres, *Westering Women*, 238–70; Paula Petrik, "Capitalists With Rooms," *Montana, the Magazine of Western History* 32 (April, 1981): 28–41.

6. Susan Armitage, "Housework and Childrearing on the Frontier: The Oral History Record," *Sociology and Social Research* 63 (April, 1979): 467–74; John Mack Faragher, "History From the Inside-out: Writing the History of Women in Rural America," *American Quarterly* 33 (Winter, 1981): 537–57.

7. For an idea of the different approaches and sometimes different opinions on women's reactions to life on the frontier, the reader should consult John Mack Faragher, *Women and Men on the Overland Trail* (New Haven: Yale University Press, 1979); Lillian Schlissel, *Women's Diaries of the Westward Journey* (New York: Schocken Books, 1982) and her "Frontier Families: Crisis in Ideology," in Sam B. Girgus, ed., *The American Self: Myth, Ideology, and Popular Culture* (Albuquerque: University of New Mexico Press, 1981), 155–65; Myres, *Westering Women*; Jeffrey, *Frontier Women*; Elizabeth Hampsten, *Read This Only to Yourself: The Private Writings of Midwestern Women, 1880–1910* (Bloomington: Indiana University Press, 1982).

8. Jeffrey, *Frontier Women*, 79–106.

9. Marion S. Goldman, *Gold Diggers and Silver Miners: Prostitution and Social Life on the Comstock Lode* (Ann Arbor: University of Michigan Press, 1981); Elizabeth Jameson, "Imperfect Unions: Class and Gender in Cripple Creek, 1894–1904," in Milton Canter and Bruce Laurie, eds., *Class, Sex, and the Woman Worker* (Westport: Greenwood Press, 1977), 166–202.

10. Sylvia Van Kirk, *Many Tender Ties: Women in Fur-Trade Society, 1670–*

1870 (Winnipeg: Watson and Dwyer Publishing, 1980); Jennifer S. H. Brown, *Strangers in Blood: Fur Trade Company Families in Indian Country* (Vancouver: University of British Columbia Press, 1980); William R. Swagerty, "Marriage and Settlement Patterns of Rocky Mountain Trappers and Traders," *Western Historical Quarterly* 11 (April, 1980): 159–80.

11. Jane Dysart, "Mexican Women in San Antonio, 1830–1860: The Assimilation Process," *Western Historical Quarterly* 7 (October, 1976): 365–75; Darlis Miller, "Cross-Cultural Marriages in the Southwest: The New Mexico Experience, 1846–1900," *New Mexico Historical Review* 57 (October, 1982): 335–59; Albert L. Hurtado, "'Hardly a Farm House—a Kitchen without Them': Indian and White Households on the California Borderland Frontier in 1860," *Western Historical Quarterly* 13 (July, 1982): 245–70; Rebecca McDowell Craver, *The Impact of Intimacy: Mexican-Anglo Intermarriage in New Mexico, 1821–1846* (El Paso: Texas Western Press, 1982).

12. For an introduction to the issues and bibliography of immigrant settlement in the West, see Frederick C. Luebke, "Ethnic Minority Groups in the American West" in Malone ed., *Historians and the American West*, 387–413, and Moses Rischin, "Beyond the Great Divide: Immigration and the Last Frontier," *Journal of American History* 55 (June, 1968): 42–53.

13. For a selection of only a few recent studies on ethnic settlement of the West, the reader might consult Frederick C. Luebke, ed., *Ethnicity on the Great Plains* (Lincoln: University of Nebraska Press, 1980); R. A. Burchell, *The San Francisco Irish, 1848–1880* (Berkeley: University of California Press, 1980); Andrew F. Rolle, *The Immigrant Upraised: Italian Adventurers and Colonists in an Expanding America* (Norman: University of Oklahoma Press, 1968); Patrick Joseph Blessing, "West among Strangers: Irish Migration to California, 1850 to 1880," (Ph.D. diss., University of California, Los Angeles, 1977); Loren B. Chan, "The Chinese in Nevada: An Historical Survey, 1856–1970," *Nevada Historical Society Quarterly* 25 (Winter, 1982): 266–314; Heather S. Hatch, "The Chinese in the Southwest," *Journal of Arizona History* 21 (Autumn, 1980): 257–74; James A. Dowie, "Unge Man, Ga Westerhut (Young Man Go Westward)," *Nebraska History* 54 (Spring, 1973): 47–63; Barbara Young, "The Nikkei in Oregon, 1834–1940," *Oregon Historical Quarterly* 76 (September, 1975): 225–57; Dale C. Maluy, "Boer Colonization in the Southwest," *New Mexico Historical Review* 52 (April, 1977): 93–110; James M. Kedre, "Czechs and Slovaks in Colorado, 1860–1920," *Colorado Magazine* 54 (Spring, 1977): 93–125; Theodore Saloutos, "Cultural Persistence and Change: Greeks in the Great Plains and the Rocky Mountain Region: 1890–1970," *Pacific Historical Review* 49 (February, 1980): 77–103.

14. Mary Wincklanovich Hart, "Merchant and Miner: Two Serbs in Early Bisbee," *Journal of Arizona History* 21 (Autumn, 1980): 313–34; Adam S. Eterovich, *Yugoslavs in Nevada, 1859–1900* (San Francisco: R. and E. Research Associates, 1973).

15. For an introduction to the bibliography and approaches to the study of the urban West, the reader should consider Bradford Luckingham, "The City in the Westward Movement—A Bibliographical Note," *Western Historical Quarterly* 5 (July, 1974): 295–306, and by the same author, "The Urban Dimension of Western History," in Malone, ed. *Historians and the American West*, 323–43; Ronald L. Davis, "Western Urban Development: A Critical Analysis," in Jerome O. Steffen, ed., *The American West: New Perspectives, New Dimensions* (Norman: University

of Oklahoma Press, 1979), 175–96; Lawrence H. Larsen, *The Urban West at the End of the Frontier* (Lawrence: Regents Press of Kansas, 1978); J. Christopher Schnell and Patrick E. McLean, "Why the Cities Grew: A Historiographical Essay on Western Urban Growth, 1850–1880," *Bulletin of the Missouri Historical Society* 27 (April, 1972): 162–77; Gunther Barth, *Instant Cities: Urbanization and the Rise of San Francisco and Denver* (New York: Oxford University Press, 1975); John W. Reps, *Cities of the American West: A History of Frontier Urban Planning* (Princeton: Princeton University Press, 1979); Robert V. Hine, *Community on the American Frontier: Separate but Not Alone* (Norman: University of Oklahoma Press, 1980).

16. Samuel Bowles, *Our New West* (Hartford, Conn.: Hartford Publishing Co., 1869), v.

17. The phrase is from Gerald D. Nash, *The American West in the Twentieth Century: A Short History of an Urban Oasis* (Englewood Cliffs: Prentice Hall, Inc., 1973).

18. Michael C. Steiner, "The Significance of Turner's Sectional Thesis," *Western Historical Quarterly* 10 (October, 1979): 437–66; Jensen, "On Modernizing Frederick Jackson Turner;" Billington, *Frederick Jackson Turner*, 364–85, 465–71.

19. Walter Prescott Webb, *The Great Plains* (Boston: Ginn and Company, 1931), vi, 8.

20. D. W. Meinig, *Southwest: Three Peoples in Geographical Change, 1600–1970* (New York: Oxford University Press, 1971), and *The Great Columbia Plain: A Historical Geography, 1805–1910* (Seattle: University of Washington Press, 1968); David J. Weber, *The Mexican Frontier, 1821–1846: The American Southwest under Mexico* (Albuquerque: University of New Mexico Press, 1982); Terry G. Jordan, *German Seed in Texas Soil: Immigrant Farmers in Nineteenth Century Texas* (Austin: University of Texas Press, 1966); Richard V. Francaviglia, *The Mormon Landscape: Existence, Creation, and Perception of a Unique Image in the American West* (New York: A.M.C. Press, Inc., 1978); Richard White, *The Roots of Dependency: Subsistence, Environment, and Social Change among the Choctaws, Pawnees, and Navajos* (Lincoln: University of Nebraska Press, 1983).

21. William H. Goetzmann, "That Awesome Space in Time," in E. Richard Hart, ed., *That Awesome Space* (Salt Lake City: Westwater Press, Inc., 1981), 55–60.

22. Nash, *The American West in the Twentieth Century*, remains the only survey of the subject.

23. Walter Prescott Webb, *Divided We Stand: The Crisis of a Frontierless Democracy* (New York: Farrar and Rinehart, Inc., 1937).

24. Walter Prescott Webb, "The American West: Perpetual Mirage," *Harper's Magazine* (May, 1957): 25–31.

25. Bernard L. Weinstein and Robert E. Firestine, *Regional Growth and Decline in the United States: The Rise of the Sunbelt and the Decline of the Northeast* (New York: Praeger Publishers, 1978), 28–30.

26. Leonard J. Arrington, *The Changing Economic Structure of the Mountain West, 1850–1950* (Logan: Utah State University Press, 1963), 39–44.

27. Ibid., 22–25; Neil Morgan, *Westward Tilt: The American West Today* (New York: Random House, 1963), 27–41; Nash, *The American West in the Twentieth Century*, 217–68; Donald J. Bogue and Calvin L. Beale, *Economic Areas of the United States* (New York: Free Press of Glencoe, 1961); Peter Wiley and Robert

Gottlieb, *Empires in the Sun: The Rise of the New American West* (New York: G. P. Putnam's Sons, 1982); Earl S. Pomeroy, *The Pacific Slope: A History of California, Oregon, Washington, Utah, and Nevada* (New York: Knopf, 1965).

28. Weinstein and Firestine, *Regional Growth and Decline*, 34–35; Michael J. Greenwood, *Migration and Economic Growth in the United States: National, Regional, and Metropolitan Perspectives* (New York: Academic Press, 1981), 30–31.

29. Richard E. Cohen, "The Geopolitical Tides," *National Journal*, October 29, 1983, 2277.

30. For a summary of the issues and current bibliography on western politics in the twentieth century, see F. Alan Coombs, "Twentieth-Century Politics," in Malone, ed., *Historians and the American West*, 300–22.

31. Gene M. Gressley examines perceptively the issues of western colonialism in two articles, "Colonialism and the American West," in his *The Twentieth Century West—A Potpourri* (Columbia: University of Missouri Press, 1977), chapter 1, and "Regionalism and the Twentieth Century West," in Steffen, ed., *The American West*, 197–234.

32. Norris Hundley, Jr., *Water and the West: The Colorado River Compact and the Politics of Water in the American West* (Berkeley: University of California Press, 1975).

33. For a summary of developments on the issue of arid lands, see W. Eugene Hollon, "Walter Prescott Webb's Arid West: Four Decades Later," in Philp and West, eds., *Essays on Walter Prescott Webb*, 53–72.

34. Earl Pomeroy, "Toward a Reorientation of Western History: Continuity and Environment," *Mississippi Valley Historical Review* 41 (March, 1955): 579–600; Howard R. Lamar, "Persistent Frontier: The West in the Twentieth Century," *Western Historical Quarterly* 4 (January, 1973), 5–25; John Caughey, "The Insignificance of the Frontier in American History, or 'Once Upon a Time There Was an American West,'" *Western Historical Quarterly* 5 (January, 1974): 5–16. The author would like to thank Mr. Jack August of Arizona State University for allowing him to read his thoughtful paper, "Recent Interpretations of the Twentieth Century West," given at the convention of the Western History Association in October, 1983.

35. Henry Nash Smith, *Virgin Land: The American West as Symbol and Myth* (Cambridge: Harvard University Press, 1950).

36. For examples of a few of the most influential treatments of the origins and earliest expressions of the western myth, see Richard Slotkin, *Regeneration through Violence: The Mythology of the American Frontier, 1600–1860* (Middletown, Conn.: Wesleyan University Press, 1973); Leo Marx, *The Machine in the Garden: Technology and the Pastoral Ideal in America* (New York: Oxford University Press, 1964); Roderick Nash, *Wilderness and the American Mind* (New Haven: Yale University Press, 1967); Kent Ladd Steckmesser, *The Western Hero in History and Legend* (Norman: University of Oklahoma Press, 1965); Rush Welter, "The Frontier West as Image of American Society, 1776–1860," *Pacific Northwest Quarterly* 52 (1961): 1–6; Bruce A. Rosenberg, *Custer and the Epic of Defeat* (University Park: University of Pennsylvania Press, 1974); Richard W. B. Lewis, *The American Adam: Innocence, Tragedy, and Tradition in the Nineteenth Century* (Chicago: University of Chicago Press, 1955); Stephen Tatum, *Inventing Billy the Kid: Visions of the Outlaw in America, 1881 to 1981* (Albuquerque: University of New Mexico Press, 1982).

37. Ray Allen Billington, *Land of Savagery, Land of Promise: The European Image of the American Frontier* (New York: W. W. Norton, 1981); Durand Eceverria, *Mirage in the West: A History of the French Image of American Society to 1815* (Princeton: Princeton University Press, 1957); Stephen Tatum, "'A Picture Gallery Unrivalled of Its Kind': Blackwood's American Frontier and the Idea of Democracy," *Western Historical Quarterly* 14 (January, 1983): 29–48; Meredith McClain, "'Der Cowboy':A Look at the German Fascination with the Wild West," *Heritage of the Great Plains* 14 (Fall, 1981): 3–12; Kenneth S. Nolley, "The Western As Jidai-Geki," *Western American Literature* 11 (Fall, 1976): 231–38.

38. Jack G. Nachbar, *Western Films: An Annotated Critical Bibliography* (New York: Garland Publishing, Inc., 1975), brings together most of the astonishing numbers of books and articles on the celluloid Western before 1975. Since then several other important works have appeared, among them Will Wright, *Six Guns and Society: A Structural Study of the Western* (Berkeley: University of California Press, 1975); John Tuska, *The Filming of the West* (Garden City: Doubleday and Co., 1976); and John H. Lenihan, *Showdown: Confronting Modern America in the Western Film* (Urbana: University of Illinois Press, 1980).

39. On various aspects of the western myth in popular culture, see Michael T. Marsden, "The Popular Western Novel as a Cultural Artifact," *Arizona and the West* 20 (Autumn, 1978): 203–14; Donald J. Mrozek, "The Image of the West in American Sport," *Journal of the West* 17 (July, 1978): 3–14; Brenda Berkman, "The Vanishing Race: Conflicting Images of the American Indian in Children's Literature, 1880–1930," *North Dakota Quarterly* 44 (Spring, 1970): 31–40; Don D. Walker, "Criticism of the Cowboy Novel: Retrospect and Reflections," *Western American Literature* 11 (Winter, 1977): 275–96; Joseph C. Porter, "The End of the Trail: The American West of Dashiell Hammett and Raymond Chandler," *Western Historical Quarterly* 6 (October, 1975): 411–24; Richard Aquila, "Images of the American West in Rock Music," *Western Historical Quarterly* 11 (October, 1980): 415–32; Jack Shadoian, "Yuh Got Pecos! Doggone, Belle, Yuh're as Good as Two Men," *Journal of Popular Culture* 12 (Spring, 1979): 721–36.

40. Nixon is quoted in Clifford P. Westermeier, "The Cowboy and Sex," in Charles W. Harris and Buck Rainey, eds., *The Cowboy: Six-Shooters, Songs, and Sex* (Norman: University of Oklahoma Press, 1976), 97. See also G. Edward White, *The Eastern Establishment and the Western Experience: The West of Frederic Remington, Theodore Roosevelt, and Owen Wister* (New Haven: Yale University Press, 1968); Donald K. Pickens, "Westward Expansion and the End of American Exceptionalism: Sumner, Turner, and Webb," *Western Historical Quarterly* 12 (October, 1981): 417.

41. John R. Milton, *The Novel of the American West* (Lincoln: University of Nebraska Press, 1980); Richard W. Etulain, *Western American Literature: A Bibliography of Interpretive Books and Articles* (Vermillion, S.D.: Dakota Press, 1972); Edwin Fussell, *Frontier: American Literature and the American West* (Princeton: Princeton University Press, 1965); William T. Pilkington, *My Blood's Country: Studies in Southwestern Literature* (Fort Worth: Texas Christian University Press, 1973); Robert Edson Lee, *From West to East: Studies in the Literature of the American West* (Urbana: University of Illinois Press, 1966); James K. Folsom, *The American Western Novel* (New Haven: Yale University Press, 1966); Fred Erisman and Richard W. Etulain, eds., *Fifty Western Writers: A Bio-bibliographical Source Book* (Westport: Greenwood Press, 1982); Richard W. Etulain, "The American Lit-

erary West and Its Interpreters: The Rise of a New Historiography," *Pacific Historical Review* 45 (August, 1976): 311–48; Robert H. Walker, "The Poets Interpret the Western Frontier," *Mississippi Valley Historical Review* 47 (March, 1961): 619–35; Richard W. Etulain, "Shifting Interpretations of Western Cultural History," in Malone, ed., *Historians and the American West*, 414–32.

   42. Webb, "History as High Adventure," 206.

   43. T. K. Whipple, *Study Out the Land* (Berkeley: University of California Press, 1943), 65.

ANNE M. BUTLER *and* RICHARD A. BAKER

Walter Prescott Webb: The Legacy

WHEN Walter Prescott Webb died on March 8, 1963, many of to-day's college students had not yet been born. Surely they must wonder why each year the history department of the University of Texas at Arlington honors Webb with a lecture series. How can they possibly feel any involvement with this professor, whose name is but a dim echo of some earlier era?[1]

Their perplexity is entirely understandable. When Walter Prescott Webb, a distinguished scholar of his day, passed away, a saddened world paused and noted, but then, ever consumed with the business of making yet more history, that world moved rapidly forward. A frenetic society turned to more dramatic events—a rash of political assassinations, a rush of civil rights protests, a scramble for space supremacy, a flurry of oddly timed fuel shortages, and a perpetual repetition of international standoffs. Had students taken the time to search the writings of Walter Webb, they could have found warnings of such events—perhaps not always explicitly stated, but his vision is there—and he would hardly have been startled by the political and historical tides that have shaped this generation.

A popular idiom dismisses everything from broken personal relationships to people as "history." "I'm history," "you're history," "that's history" punctuate trendy conversations on campuses across the nation. It is the collegiate nod to the fleeting, temporary America that races from what is "now" to what is "in," where tomorrow promises a new assortment of fads and fancies to be acquired and discarded with equal haste. Certainly, in both the real and the trendy definitions, Walter Prescott Webb is "history." Those who knew him grow older themselves, and their struggle to instill this annual commemoration with meaning and zest perhaps wearies even his most devoted associates. Each year the purpose must seem more vague and remote. After all, how long can an academic community realistically retain its attachment to a personality absent from its midst for more than twenty years?

The ultimate rebuke to the significance of one teacher, to the endurance of one personality, struck in 1983. Exactly twenty years after the death of Walter Prescott Webb, widely acclaimed in his lifetime as one of the outstanding intellectuals and educators of the twentieth century, *Time* magazine replaced its honored "Man of the Year" award with the computer as "Machine of the Year." On that occasion, America's slick news weekly enthusiastically proclaimed, "Several human candidates might have represented 1982, but none symbolized the past year more richly, or will be viewed by history as more significant, than a machine: the computer."[2] Six months later, Anne Arundel Community College in Maryland invited a 5-foot 2-inch, 175-pound computer named Robot Redford to give the commencement address. Administrators explained that the purpose was to draw attention to new programs in computer science and technology and not to seek sensational publicity. Accordingly, the robot marched in the opening procession but did not dress in academic regalia.[3] Surely, nothing underscores the change in American education more than the machine's entry into the classroom. What began as a simple use of tape recorders in language labs has mushroomed into a full-scale computer curriculum; more than 100,000 computers are now in American schools. A technology that once served to facilitate campus registration and billing procedures now extends to the instructional level in all areas of American education. Not only university and secondary institutions, but even elementary school corridors ring with the new terminology of "on-line searching," "retrieval systems," "floppy disks," and "memory banks." Parents with a worried eye on the destiny of American public education scurry for the latest in home equipment so their preschoolers can get the jump on computer literacy. More and more students unquestioningly accept the infallibility of the machine, confident that it alone is the rational and rapid approach to a sound education.

In this world of technical wizardry, where the process of thoughtful inquiry is often replaced by mechanical proficiency, it is useful to dust off the memory of Walter Prescott Webb and to bask in the absolute subjectivity and total intellectual immersion he brought to education. To bring his memory into sharper focus, recollections of two of his former students provide a physical image of Webb. John Haller first encountered him in the 1940s in Webb's course on the American frontier. As Haller entered the classroom he saw "a short bulky man with a very large, very round head, no visible neck, owl-like eyes, and paunchy cheeks; with a grave preoccupied air and slow, deliberate movements. Seated at his desk," Haller continued, "he spoke in a measured resonant, impressive tone, quite lacking in Texas drawl, distinguished rather by a richly cultured quality difficult to define but impossible to mistake."[4] A few years later, Frank Vandiver observed that Webb's appearance affected students in different ways. For Vandiver, the teacher's scowl instilled momentary fear. He noted that Webb "had a proper height, was taller than his slight forward stoop indicated, gazed steadily from slightly squinted, sometimes watery eyes, and his weathered face told him an outdoorsman." Vandiver continued that Webb favored "a Texas businessman's Stetson—a kind of five gallon compromise with the Old West . . . liked simple clothes, and stuck generally to the same style suits, plainly cut and without stripes or designs."[5]

This teacher did not parade about his campus, detached and secure in the possession of sanitized formulas and easy solutions. Webb personified the opposite. From his earliest teaching days, he plunged into his students' lives with a fervor born not of the crusading intruder, but of the inspiring mentor and friend. His was a highly personalized, fiercely spirited understanding of the dynamics between teacher and student. He lived to the fullest his conviction that a teacher's success rested on the need and ability to inject students with lively intellectual concerns. He viewed the professorial role as the responsibility to invigorate, to challenge, to scold students into a better appreciation of their own intellectual prowess. At the same time, Webb relentlessly demanded the same return for himself from his students, for above all else he perceived that without this healthy interaction teachers risked scholarly decay at the hands of their own intellectual stagnation and arrogance.[6]

Webb delineated the value of this dual role in his explanation of the historical seminar. For his students, Webb saw the seminar director as the master craftsman, trying to make master craftsmen out of apprentices and journeymen, putting them through the historian's tasks of reading, collecting, analyzing, organizing, and writing. For himself, a seminar director "is trying to push out the bounds of knowledge. He has gone far enough to ask questions, to know what kind to ask, but he has not found the answers. Therefore," continued Webb, "he calls in a group of graduate students, already equipped with method, takes them as junior partners, and sets them off on a quest for the answers to his questions. He is seeking aid while giving it." Shifting to a rustic analogy, Webb likened the seminar director to the leader of a crew of axemen, hunters, scouts, and observers. "The library is the high mountain and the forested valley where inspiring views and depressing confusion alternate," while "the seminar table is the campfire where the party gathers and each member reports what he has seen and what he thinks about it." He concluded that successful seminars, conducted by curious, restless investigators, "bold enough to build a program of inquiry and writing around a compelling idea," existed only as long as there was that "compelling idea." For Webb, "if there was no idea, there was no seminar."[7]

Webb conducted two major seminars during his career at the University of Texas; each resulted in a major book, and each ended with the book's publication. The first began on a rainy February night shortly after World War I. While preparing an article on the Texas Rangers, Webb was struck with a "moment of insight and synthesis" that placed all his previous research on the topic into a meaningful pattern. In thinking of the Colt revolver, Webb suddenly realized that it was the product of man's move from the forest into an open, treeless plain. He wondered what other changes had taken place as a result of that transition. When he found that no one else could answer that question to his satisfaction, he decided to offer a course on the Great Plains. As he later joked, "I did not rate a seminar, and I did not know enough to lecture."[8] So he simply told his class, "I think something important happened to ideas and institutions when men left the woodland to live on the plains in middle America. Will you help me find out what happened to this and that and the other?" He admitted that he "surreptitiously converted this class, and succeeding ones, into a seminar—into hunting answers to my questions."[9]

In 1938, Webb initiated the seminar that led to publication, fourteen years later, of *The Great Frontier*. Conceived in Webb's desire to follow the frontier concept to its logical conclusion, that work focused on the impact that the discovery of three new continents had on established ideas and institutions at the beginning of the sixteenth century. In this, as in his earlier seminar, students responded willingly to his direction. They recognized that while he would borrow from the best of their research for his own writing, so too would he recognize and promote originality in their work. After one student had presented a promising paper on the influence of European literature on the American frontier, Webb commanded him to enlarge the paper into a book. In the ultimate compliment from teacher to student, he said, "You have the nucleus of a great book, and you have the ability to finish it. You write it and I'll see that it gets published."[10]

Webb's genius as a teacher was particularly evident in his graduate seminar, where the format of teacher and student interaction was deliberately informal and unstructured. Similarly, his teaching brilliance emerged when students encountered him sitting in his office or walking from Garrison Hall across campus to the Night Hawk or the Driskill Hotel. In a crowded undergraduate lecture hall, however, that genius emerged more slowly. One student recalled that Webb "lectured from notes, with the corners of his mouth turned down as if he were not particularly enjoying what he was doing. It has been my impression," the student continued, "that he did not care to speak before large groups of people, nor did he like to get very far from written copy. He had the information and he knew how to impart the maximum in fifty minutes; he did not consider himself an entertainer and he made no use of attention-catching tricks or gadgets."[11]

Nonetheless, Webb remained intensely concerned with the quality of undergraduate history training throughout his career. In 1956 he set forth a long-range plan for the University of Texas history department to assist it in meeting "a crisis which it has not faced before." Webb viewed with alarm the "tidal wave" of students that was rapidly approaching the nation's universities as a result of increased birth rates and the greater percentage of young people seeking a higher education. Webb feared that the onslaught of new students would result in an erosion of academic standards and a flood of ill-prepared teachers into high school and college classrooms. He urged the university administration to resist the trend of hiring more junior faculty and of paying senior members increasingly mediocre wages. Instead, he counselled that the university emphasize faculty productivity. Senior professors, in teaching large classes, should be given "enough assistance to relieve them of detailed drudgery. Their business would be to teach. They should," in Webb's view, "have the same quality of help that is given to a surgeon, a lawyer, or a business executive." This, he believed, would ensure that undergraduates would not have to wait until later in their university careers before making contact with eminent scholars.[12]

Webb believed that historians at the University of Texas had an obligation not only to their beginning undergraduates but also to the state's high school teachers of history and, through them, to their students. He lamented the intrusion of the social studies "methodologists" into high school history teaching and the resultant lowering of standards. In response to this situation, the university, in Webb's opinion, had simply "abdicated and retired to the cloister."[13]

Webb felt that students everywhere should be exposed to brilliant teaching of history. Late in his life he received a Ford Foundation grant of $91,300 for "American Civilization by the Interpreters," a series of televised lectures by twenty eminent American historians. Aimed at upper-division undergraduates and graduate students, the lectures would allow each of the selected master historians to set "forth his point of view about American history, telling the students what he tried to do in his writing, and finally giving them what he considers the best of his contribution." Along the way, Webb encountered resistance from those unwilling to consider new technological applications for teaching and from those who felt his budget was inadequate. Historian Samuel Eliot Morison told Webb that he liked everything about the plan except the time and the fee. "Twenty-seven minutes is too short and $300 too little for a proper lecture—especially in Texas where you have plenty of both," said Morison. Yet even this Harvard academic recognized the essential soundness in Webb's teaching goals.[14]

Clearly, it was through this philosophy of teaching that Webb made his greatest contribution to American education. His prize-winning books and his distinguished professional posts are impressive and noteworthy, but it was Walter Webb's profound and lasting impact on his students that earns for him his well-deserved reputation as an educator of excellence. If modern students can grasp some measure of Webb's importance as a teacher, they will appreciate this commemorative series more and will be better equipped—even those who never knew him—to return to their computer terminals determined to protect that which the machines threaten: intellectual curiosity, scholarly individuality, and educational passion.

Shortly after Webb's death, his closest associates and former students decided to ensure that his most cherished educational values be perpetuated in the form of this lecture series. Such a forum promised not only to gather together prominent scholars to honor Webb, but more importantly to provide a vehicle for reminding later generations of students that from the dusty plains of West Texas had come one of the really remarkable minds of the twentieth century. He had emerged not only to lead Texans to a richer understanding of their historical development but to articulate important human ideas for the nation and, indeed, the world.

To that end, Webb did not seek out the academic elites, a group for whom he had ill-concealed scorn. Rather, he directed his energies toward his students at the university. Year after year, Walter Webb looked across his desk and into the faces of the unsophisticated, untrained youth of the Lone Star State. Drawn from the towns, the hamlets, the farms of Texas, dropped at the entrance of the admissions building with a stern parental command, "Make something of yourself!" these novice scholars were to be Webb's sounding boards for the refinement of his ideas and the birth of their own. To launch these academic neophytes, Webb first exorcised their destructive self-evaluation that denigrated their own rural origins as intellectual impediments. Under Webb's piercing tutelage, students awakened to the notion that thinking is man's universal experience. Whether from the South Texas brush along the Nueces, the flat open Panhandle plains close to the Canadian, or the densely forested Piney Woods region near the Angelina, all learned the error in making an intellectual apology for the place called "home." Webb, who not only arose from the parched fields around Ranger but synthesized that experience into a regional vision, understood that Texas students from Guthrie, Sonora, or Crockett need never stand in the intellectual shadow of anyone. The universality of human thinking accorded mankind everywhere the same intellectual rights; the privileges of thought and the excitement of creativity were not the special domain of any one country, region, or collection of academicians.

That a poor farm lad who had struggled and scratched for years to secure his own formal education could apply such a concept to himself was mark enough for one lifetime, but Webb's greatness lay in his dynamic ability to convey the idea to his students, thus freeing them from the constraints of their own self-prejudices. Walter Webb armed his students with the most critical of academic weapons—the confidence to push their own intellectual resources to the limits of curiosity, creativity, and thoughtfulness. He gave to his students the realization that they had the right to enter the community of thinkers as peers, standing in deference to no person or group.

But Walter Prescott Webb was not a kindly, meek Mr. Chips type who gently guided his students to a utopian world of the intellect. Walter Webb had a more complex and compelling nature, not easily dismissed as just another plaster-coated saint whose virtues are to be extolled without a glimmer of a fault. Throughout his academic life, Webb was a curious blend of opposites. He could be the gentleman of unmatchable wit and charm, but when angered, he could maintain an unfaltering and unforgiving demeanor. Nonetheless, long-held animosities could melt in the warmth of an unexpected embrace from an old foe. He cherished exchanges with close friends and the hearty mirth of a good joke, but if he felt abused, he could be petty and mean-spirited. He knew ambition, had a keen distaste for poverty, and feared failure. He drove himself to be productive, but he remained disorganized and careless about small details. He cultivated his own pride and enjoyed the international prestige he won from his writings and lectures, yet he suffered from frightful depression and mental exhaustion that threatened his physical well-being.[15]

He was in all these things a man of enormous personal passion who turned the full heat of that fire upon his work and his students. As such, he was remarkable, not because of his perfections, but because the totality of his essence became the living embodiment of history, that most passionate of disciplines.

Webb had no patience with the traditional practices that caused history to be labeled a deadly dull subject, forced upon students like a hateful dose of castor oil. For Webb, history thundered a symphonic beauty across the world, paused in each environment, each culture, to play its rhapsody, then swept on to a new area with its composition enriched. He directed his students to find new harmonies, to write new passages as well. Some would do so with greater vigor and determination than others, but all had the opportunity to march through this unusually eloquent fantasia with this intensely personal conductor. The intellectual exchange between teacher and student had within it the seeds of discord, for in Webb's greatest service to his students—the unleashing of their intellectual creativity—he inadvertently placed himself in competition with them. He thrust students onto his stage, where they responded with the independence that he fired in them. The result was that Webb, ever a dominant and forceful personality, never fell into the rut of static relationships with students. For good or ill, his own spirit circumscribed his associations with students for more than forty years.

His first adventures in teaching brought him to a succession of rural schools throughout Texas. In each, his innovative techniques and his willingness to throw himself into all community activities earned the admiration of students still subjected to methods from the nineteenth century. Webb, quick-witted and clever, cast off the dullness of learning by rote and introduced a variety of approaches and projects to capture the imaginations of his youthful charges. He did not shy away from a new notion or from techniques he had observed in his own schooling at the university. Ultimately, he would be remembered for his zesty encouragement of each individual's talents and interests and his refusal to pressure his classes to fit any one stereotypical mold. Webb certainly expanded the horizons of his students, and in so doing he kept himself intellectually vibrant as he moved from one tiny community to the next.[16]

His eager flocks surely never realized the emotional and physical toll the experience exacted on their young teacher. Despite his energy and cleverness in the classroom, Webb fretted about himself and his future. His lifelong emotional fervor and anxiety caused him long hours of introspection as he tried to unriddle the best future for himself. No cloying do-gooder, Webb chafed under the heavy demands of being teacher, athletic coach, community lecturer, and PTA chief, and he disliked the restrictions and regulations of administrators. He plotted continuously for ways to secure the necessary funds to complete his own education at the University of Texas. In a burst of absolute honesty, he declared, "Teaching is little short of pure drudgery, especially when it comes to the paper grading and bookkeeping part of it."[17]

Completion of his undergraduate degree and the promise of a permanent post did not dissolve Webb's uncertainty about his future in the teaching profession. By 1915, his strong sense of ambition and his weariness of a lifetime of debt began to lure him from the realm of chalk and erasers to a possibly more lucrative career in business. He rationalized his decision, saying that he was "sick of school work on starvation wages," and found the "empty honor of teaching had lost its allurement for me."[18]

In 1918, this gifted leader of students left the classroom and began a job as bookkeeper. Fortunately for generations of students, it proved to be only a brief detour, for in the fall of that year, the University of Texas history department offered Webb a position training history teachers. Webb, whose own experiences in the country schools of Texas had convinced him of the need for innovative methods in history instruction, readily accepted. Thus began an era at the University of Texas in which this one professor placed an indelible imprint on the direction of education, not only in his own state but across the nation.

At the University of Texas, Webb freely vented his inclination to stress ideas and to watch the subsequent blossoming of new concepts in the minds of his students. In all things, Webb longed for students to work independently and to think grandly. Some fell short of the mark, confused and unsure if not strictly led through routine course work in a traditional fashion. They dropped by the wayside, grumbling about Webb's inadequacies and lack of direction. A few others recognized that they were under the hand of a master teacher, but shy and insecure, they never really knew how to take advantage of his brilliance. They departed changed but aware that they had missed some part of the Webb equation.

Others, though sometimes as uncertain of how to chart the way through Webb's complex and often gruff personality, nonetheless plunged on, delighted by the challenges he offered and anxious to extract the most from each encounter with him. Some worked closely with him after their university days; others moved on, keenly intrigued by the way this one professor had brought a kaleidoscope of ideas to their minds. Many have continued to implant his values in American life. Among them, to be sure, are those whose names are not famous but who have diligently attacked vacuity and ignorance in all corners of American society. Others are among the nation's educational luminaries, the finest representatives of academic achievement. They are indeed a star-studded collection—these editors, teachers, journalists, businessmen, historians, executive directors, and ranchers. Their diverse professions, their very lives, form a perpetual reminder of Webb's unflagging devotion to his basic educational philosophy and his tireless endeavors to convince his students of the merits and range of the human intellect.

Despite the magnitude of his notions, despite his far-reaching and singular influence on students, despite the intention of this lecture series to honor Webb, this annual symposium in its first decade repeatedly bypassed a direct testimonial to Webb's greatest gift to the nation—his scholarly protégés. Conference sessions ranged across a broad spectrum of subjects from the American Civil War to Russian intellectual history, from the Gilded Age to radicalism in contemporary America. Each year, a significant conference and publication resulted from these topics, but not one of them acknowledged the ultimate Webb product, his students. In part, of course, explanation for this omission rests with the conference organizers, themselves often the students of Webb, who certainly had no desire to twist this occasion into an exercise of self-congratulation. Rather, they did exactly as Webb would have expected them to do; they developed lecture topics centered on important historical epics.

It was not until the tenth annual lecture that Walter Webb himself became the focal point for the commentators, each a former Webb student. The product of that April, 1975, conference is a slim volume of essays written by a handful of his students.[19] Of Webb's likely response to the book, frontier historian Ray Allen Billington said, "He would have gloried in the fact that scholars have been expanding the trails that he blazed . . ."[20]

Yet, this book reflects more than merely a tribute to the memory of a beloved teacher. It illuminates the professional commitment of the essayists themselves. Each of them, through his own career, has exhibited some special Webb quality. These essays and the historians who wrote them help us to hear again Webb's battle cry to the profession—strive mightily and always for imagination, creativity, and independence of mind.

Joe B. Frantz's essay, "Walter Prescott Webb and the South," etches the pattern of Webb's almost latent sense of South and then traces the reemergence of Webb's interest in his home region later in his life.[21] Frantz understands the southern hues in Webb as perhaps no other scholar has, but beyond this, his essay defines the very essence of "southernness," not just for Walter Webb but for all who spring from her land. Frantz's work on the South, especially through its frontier era, touches on government, economics, social life, and philosophy with such bold strokes that students, historians, and even politicians know they have encountered one who understands not only his region but its importance to the nation. Accordingly, he is the heir apparent to the regional concerns so forcefully stated by Walter Webb. Using his southern heritage as an intellectual thesis, Frantz, in the Webb volume and throughout his career, has been the living symbol of Webb's insistence on imaginative, captivating style. Whether writing or speaking, Joe Frantz snares his audience with his cleverness, leads them with his deftly turned phrases, and sure-footedly draws them to his points. He has made the trip so pleasant with his warm and easy manner that listeners are suddenly jolted into realizing that this Texan, like his teacher before him, expects people to think.

The second essay of the 1975 lecture series is W. Turrentine Jackson's "Australians and the Comparative Frontier."[22] In this paper, Jackson displays the Webb love for the creative and the academic linkage between teacher and student. A creative Webb grandly applied the Turner thesis on a global basis; Jackson reapplies the ideas to an area not fully developed by Webb. The result is one of the most difficult of historical feats—an essay that uses familiar material to provide refreshing and informative new insights. Jackson's ability to connect concepts and epics is in the best Webb tradition. He avoids the label of provincialism that often—and unjustly—burdens frontier historians and produces works that interest scholars of many persuasions. Jackson's expertise in western environmental concerns, especially water policy, places him among the Webb followers who use intellectual perceptions to educate an unheeding populace to the long-range implications of conservation neglect. When he couples that knowledge with his research in other fields such as European economic investments in the West, Jackson forcefully demonstrates Webb's vision that creative minds should consistently reach for new horizons.

In the third piece, "Walter Prescott Webb's Arid West: Four Decades Later," W. Eugene Hollon reveals that straightforward independence of mind so cherished by Webb. [23] Through a review of Webb's zealous efforts to dramatize western water needs, Hollon shows that Webb not only analyzed the many-faceted societal impoverishments inflicted on the people of an arid region but tied the continuation of that human hardship to the heedless, exploitative decisions of government and industry. This sensitive topic—the future of the arid West—was perhaps the most controversial subject that Webb tackled in a career filled with contests, and his outspoken criticisms and stark warnings won him the acerbic hostility of entrepreneurs and politicians who saw ventures rich with economic promise in a twentieth-century burgeoning West. Hollon could have written a brisk account that simply retold Webb's conservation interests and the prickly disputes that followed, but he chose a bolder role: to reinforce the accuracy of Webb's perceptions with his own critique of western environmental administration since 1964. Hollon's scathing indictment of land developers for the unreasonable stress they place on western ecology, in spite of mounting geographical abuses and pollution hazards, reveals his refusal to be intimidated by glossy rhetoric or possible censure. Hollon, like Webb, will confront a modern problem from a critical, if unpopular, perspective when he argues for the future from his historical evidence.

George Wolfskill also delivered a masterful paper, "The Webb 'Great Frontier' Hypothesis and International Law," at the tenth annual Webb series.[24] Fundamental historical concerns and the implications of the emerging space frontier gave Wolfskill the springboard from which to discuss the growth of modern legal philosophy. Drawing on the ideas of Walter Webb and an array of European scholars, Wolfskill enlarged their notions to conclude that the international legal system has been transformed drastically in our own century. He questioned the ability of the present system to withstand the additional burdens and demands of tomorrow's world, where man's communities may be located on earth or in outer space. Wolfskill then charged the international community to avoid procrastination and begin the weighty task of repairing a legal structure that is already becoming obsolete. This articulate, forceful essay relates to Webb's thought but expands the ultimate vision and interpretation, revealing Wolfskill to be a fair champion of Webb's perpetual call for imaginative, thoughtful scholarship.

There is one final article in the volume published for the 1975 Webb lecture series. This selection, however, was not delivered at the symposium, nor was it written by a former Webb student. The essay, "Webb: The Schoolteacher," won the first annual Webb-Smith Prize.[25] It was written by the late Walter Rundell, Jr., to whom this 1984 lecture series is dedicated.

Walter Rundell, himself a native of a small Texas town and a graduate of the University of Texas, found Walter Webb's intellectual vision captivating. He admired Webb's commitment to vigorous thought, his insistence on hard work, and his strikingly bold ideas. Though Rundell never had a class nor studied under Webb, he became a Webb student in the fullest sense of the word. Upon his graduation from the university, Rundell intended to pursue his chosen career as music critic. Before he could do that, however, he had a military service obligation to satisfy. Here Dr. Edith Parker, a former Webb student, intervened. She had become acquainted with Rundell when they both worked in the university's music department, and she thought highly of his literary talent. Employed as an Army historian in 1953, she arranged for him to be assigned to the Army Finance Corps' World War II historical project. As Rundell later wrote Webb, "I decided that would be undoubtedly the best assignment I could get, although at the time I was not contemplating any further academic career." He continued, "My association with Dr. Parker proved to be extremely enjoyable and beneficial. It was through her that I became your 'intellectual grandchild,' as she has put it."[26]

Thirty years ago Rundell told Webb, "The thing I find most significant about your works is that you have pioneered by introducing new concepts in the social studies. Shedding new and different light on fundamental problems is to me the highest achievement of scholarship."[27] Over the next three decades Rundell, as a professional historian, transformed that high regard into twelve scholarly articles about Webb. His essays and lectures on the subject were punctuated with the very imagination, creativeness, and independence of mind that Webb longed to see permeate the historical profession. In the process, Rundell emerged as the foremost authority on Walter Webb and elevated the experiences of Texas's best known historian from mere biographical recitation to scholarly analysis. It is from the Rundell writings that others glean new appreciation for the broad scope of Webb's influence and the many facets of his brilliance.

Rundell, who had already published five major historical studies on topics ranging from military finance to the training of American historians to oil exploration, planned to make his next work an intellectual biography of Walter Webb. Unlike Webb, he was a stickler for meticulous research and pursued his projects with an orderly care for the smallest details. Consequently, in an academic investment of more than twenty-five years, Rundell gathered, arranged, and cataloged a wealth of Webb materials.[28] It is a measure of Rundell's enthusiastic dedication to the biography that when informed that he had won the first Webb-Smith Prize, his pleasure was enhanced because the announcement arrived while he was seated at his typewriter working on additional Webb projects. It was so like him that this intensely fine scholar relished the intellectual correctness of being rewarded for his labors while he yet pursued them.

Walter Rundell had a depth of talents and skills still to bring to his work on Walter Prescott Webb, and his Webb writings will have an unfinished touch because his book can never be finished quite as he would have written it. It is of course he—Walter Rundell—who should have assessed Walter Webb the educator, for no one knew the subject better. That he could not touches all who knew him with sadness. Yet even in this time of grief, this paper confirms the impact of such teachers, for Walter Rundell, much like Walter Webb before him, nurtured his students intellectually and imparted to them the academic continuity that binds the spirit of teacher and student. An intellectual lineage is not disrupted, even by the hand of death, when the gifts of education have been bestowed by such as these two Walters—Rundell and Webb.

If this survey of several noteworthy Webb students fails to convince that Webb the teacher could best the instructional machines, then it is suggested that he would have been the first to understand the technical professors that dominate education. Had classroom computers appeared during Webb's era, he would have quickly perceived the importance of using machines as intellectual tools, although he would have stoutly resisted those popular trends that use computers as a series of shallow video games for the mindless. Webb expected thinking to be an arduous, time-consuming task, and he would not have permitted his students to become vapid, high-tech button pushers, who seek problem solutions through color codes and buzz words. He would have forced students to use machines to attain new dimensions in the arena of academic exploration. Webb, unwilling to become a slave to a piece of equipment, would have mastered the machine and molded its uses for the betterment of human thought.

Webb would have tackled this new challenge, because in all things Walter Webb stood as the champion of human values and the advocate of intellectual creativity. These were his guiding beacons, and he pursued them with all his personal fiber. Webb is truly an intellectual champion because he invested both his strengths and his weaknesses in his untiring quest for knowledge. Few are so willing to expose their full humanity, to reveal the inner, personal core in the cause of human thought.

Walter Webb brought to his teaching career that rare quality of one who understands the intellectual romance of teaching. In a world that discourages emotional involvement in anything, Webb continues to stand as a professional maverick; involvement was his hallmark, and he towers above others as the passionate and moving answer to the intellectual and personal indifference that engulfs American campuses. Webb would look askance at a nation that sees education merely as a routine, temporary annoyance preliminary to degree certification, the purpose of which is entirely to ensure a job. Webb would reject that philosophy because it fails to assume a moral obligation that extends beyond the individual and encompasses not only the academic world but the human community. For Walter Webb, the personal struggle, the disappointments, the frustrations, even the glories did not excuse a thinking person from the responsibilities attached to one's intellectual obligations.

In view of Webb's commitment to education, faculties and students are challenged to rededicate themselves to the extraordinary values he personified. Such a task will demand that students set aside the aloofness and convenience of machinery to engage in the pain and struggle of academic growth. Faculty members will need to face their own human intellectual imperfections and wrestle them to a finer level of thought. In this spirit the efforts, successes, and failures of each other will give vibrance to America's academic communities. The values that Webb shared with his students will once again permeate the educational arena. If Americans will revive these once-dynamic sentiments, then their adventure in the realm of high technology will be bold and filled with the verve and excitement of creative scholars. College campuses will again become the haven of grand thinkers and the protector of the intellectual rights of all people. In so doing, all will be the guardians of the academic spirit of Walter Webb and will deserve to be called his students.

NOTES

1. The most accessible brief summary of Webb's life and writings is by Walter Rundell, Jr., in *Dictionary of American Biography*, Supp. VII, S.V. "Webb, Walter Prescott."

2. *Time*, "Machine of the Year," January 3, 1983, 12–32, 37, 39.

3. *Time*, "Nation: The Talk Circuit," May 9, 1983, 39.

4. John Haller, "A Most Generous Offer," in Ronnie Dugger, ed., *Three Men in Texas: Bedichek, Webb, and Dobie* (Austin: University of Texas Press, 1967), 93.

5. Frank L. Vandiver, "Walter Prescott Webb: Teacher," *Southwest Review* 48 (Autumn, 1963): 377.

6. Walter Prescott Webb, *An Honest Preface and Other Essays* (Boston: Houghton Mifflin, 1959), 147.

7. Walter Prescott Webb, *History as High Adventure* (Austin, Texas: Pemberton Press, 1969), 83–86, 90–91, 101. This essay also appears as "The Historical Seminar: Its Outer Shell and Its Inner Spirit" in the *Mississippi Valley Historical Review* 42 (June, 1955): 3–23.

8. *History as High Adventure*, 102–103.

9. Ibid., 103.

10. John Haller, "A Most Generous Offer," 96.

11. Wilson M. Hudson, "Webb My Teacher," in Ronnie Dugger, ed., *Three Men in Texas*, 124; W. Eugene Hollon, "Walter Prescott Webb: The Classroom Teacher," paper delivered at the annual meeting of the Western Historical Association, Hot Springs, Arkansas, October 13, 1978.

12. Walter Prescott Webb, "A Problem of the History Department," in Walter Rundell Papers, in family custody.

13. Walter Prescott Webb, "The University Historian and History Teachers," *History as High Adventure*, 106–111.

14. Walter Prescott Webb, "Proposed TV Course to be Offered by the University of Texas," [draft], Webb Papers, Box 2M254, University of Texas at Austin Archives; Samuel Eliot Morison to W. P. Webb, September 22, 1962, Webb Papers, Box 2M269.

15. Interviews by Walter Rundell, Jr., with Mary Joe Carroll, November 19, 1977; Seymour V. Connor, April 2, 1976; Robert C. Cotner, December 2, 1977; W. Turrentine Jackson, October 12, 1978; Edith H. Parker, July 14, 1975, in Rundell Papers, family custody.

16. Walter Rundell, Jr., "Webb the Schoolteacher," in Kenneth R. Philip and Elliott West, eds., *Essays on Walter Prescott Webb* (Austin: University of Texas, 1976), 95–123.

17. Ibid., 109.

18. Ibid., 114–15.

19. Philip and West, *Essays on Walter Prescott Webb*.

20. Ibid., xvii.

21. Joe B. Frantz, "Walter Prescott Webb and the South," ibid., 3–15.

22. W. Turrentine Jackson, "Australians and the Comparative Frontier," ibid., 17–51.

23. W. Eugene Hollon, "Walter Prescott Webb's Arid West: Four Decades Later," ibid., 53–72.

24. George Wolfskill, "The Webb 'Great Frontier' Hypothesis and International Law," ibid., 73–93.

25. Walter Rundell, Jr., "Webb: The Schoolteacher," ibid., 95–123.

26. Walter Rundell, Jr., to Walter Prescott Webb, April 4, 1954, Rundell Papers, family custody.

27. Ibid.

28. For a brief survey of Rundell's life and work, see William T. Hagan, "Walter Rundell, Jr." *The Western Historical Quarterly* 14 (April, 1983), 141–44.

DENNIS REINHARTZ

Teaching History with Maps:
A Graphic Dimension

THE adventurer Captain John Smith once pointed out that "history without geography is a vagrant. . . ." Historians know the verity of Smith's statement and since Herodotus have validated it through their writing and teaching. Certainly, Walter Prescott Webb was no exception. The physical environment and its impact on humanity's ideas and institutions formed the essential basis for all of his historical thinking and teaching. To Webb, maps were invaluable in elucidating the geographic factors and spatial relationships that have determined the pattern of western history over the last half a millennium. In his classes Webb used maps extensively to promote deeper student involvement in the subject matter through the graphic stimulation of their reasoning processes. For Webb maps were both tools and artifacts to help convey and enrich his visions of the past. It is most appropriate, therefore, to consider here the use of maps in making historical instruction more effective.

Maps comprise a powerful, widely used, complex, and little understood form of communication that is as old as language itself. Humanity achieved "graphicacy" even before it achieved literacy. We learned to draw before we learned to write, and we also probably mapped before we wrote. This is true not only of our prehistoric and historic ancestors but also of more contemporary preliterate peoples.

Since the late Renaissance, the unique graphic language of maps has made them important to historians as sources, representations, and teaching devices. Although the use of maps in the teaching of history is the principal concern of this essay, any discussion of this topic must also consider maps as sources in historical research and as illustrations in historical narrative. Their documentary, artifactual nature as voices from the past and their illustrative capacity make maps invaluable in the teaching of history. This essay will touch briefly on the history of cartography, maps and human development, and the traditional use of maps in social science education, then will explain maps as artifacts and graphic imagery to demonstrate their more effective use in the teaching of history.[1]

Cartography, the making of maps, evolved independently among many peoples around the world. The earliest maps are often unreadable and even unrecognizable today because there are no neolithic survivors to serve as translators. In such cases we have become the current addressees for a now unintelligible message transmitted millennia ago by an unknown sender; communication is no longer wholly or even partially possible. Similar problems exist in understanding the maps of more contemporary indigenous peoples like the North American Indians of the period before the European discovery.[2] With maps of the historic period, which often can be corroborated by other documentation, recognition, understanding, and communication increase dramatically. The earliest identifiable examples of maps are settlement plans dating back to about 6000 B.C., while the earliest known world map is from seventh-century B.C. Babylon and portrays the earth as a disk.[3] Bronze Age Mesopotamian and Egyptian maps on stone, clay tablets, and papyrus from as early as 2500 B.C. also survive.

The Greco-Egyptian scientist Claudius Ptolemy (ca. A.D. 90–160) postulated not only the cosmography of the geocentric universe but also the basis for the modern discipline of geography. Included in his legacy was a manual for mapmaking with three projections. During the Middle Ages, scholars in the West abandoned Ptolemy for Christian cartography, while in the East, scholars preserved his teachings and fused them with Indian and Islamic knowledge to further cartographic progress and expand the contemporary view of the world. By the year 1000, the Chinese were printing maps with ink on paper and using them with early examples of magnetic compasses.[4]

With the western appearance of Ptolemy's work during the early Renaissance, maps and charts took more accurate, recognizably modern forms. In the 1470s, better maps began to be printed in the West, helping accelerate the great age of European discovery and exploration while at the same time producing the means to

"Secunda etas mundi, secunda etas mūdi," Nuremberg, 1493. Ptolemaic projection. Cartographic History Library, University of Texas at Arlington.

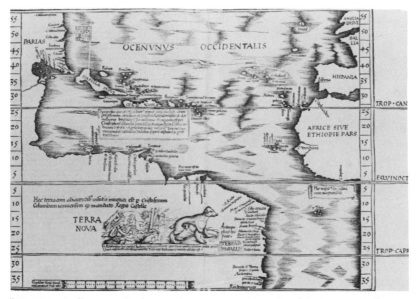

"Terra Nova," 1525. Ptolemaic projection. Cartographic History Library, University of Texas at Arlington.

record the new findings. Modern scientific and technological advancements have created maps, charts, and globes of still greater accuracy and scope, leading to the mass production of cartographic aids and their increased accessibility. Today, we continue to map not only our own shrinking planet but the expanding universe as well.[5]

Maps are significant landmarks of historical development and achievement, summarizing the scientific, technological, and intellectual strengths of an era and recording the political, economic, and social values of the times in which they were created. Since the beginning of history, they have been intimately involved in human development. They have helped people define who they are, where they are, and how they move about. Maps delineate physical, political, economic, and social features and depict the effect the environment has on us as well as our impact on the environment. In more recent times, thematic maps not only have chronicled and displayed but also disseminated and expanded human knowledge. In short, maps have helped both to record and to make history. Consequently, they have served for some time as valuable tools in the process of teaching humanity about itself and its past. Maps also can be viewed as art, part of the wider human aesthetic experience, or as postholes from which one can explore broader trends, concepts, and accomplishments. As Michael and Susan Southworth argue, "Maps can kindle the imagination, sustain trips through time and space, make real the milieux of . . . history."[6]

Many people have collected maps for antiquarian or aesthetic purposes, but historians actually use them, both in the writing and the teaching of history. No one knows for sure when maps were first employed in the teaching of history; it was probably when history was first taught. Since at least the 1590s, maps in the form of board games (of course, all board games are maps), "dissected" (jigsaw) puzzles, playing cards, and globes have been used as educational materials.[7] One of the most recent examples of these map games is a 3½-inch physical globe that operates on the principle of the often infuriating Rubik's Cube. Its description in the 1983 Christmas catalog from Pier 1 Imports reads in part: "To play, scramble the earth's oceans and continents, then restore order. An education in geography and logic."[8] In 1868 the British cartographer William

Stokes published the collapsible Stokes's Capital Mnemonical Globe, which associated familiar facial features with unfamiliar geography. Commenting on the educational value of his maps, Stokes once remarked, "A little playful pleasantry . . . will enliven the proceedings, and . . . strengthen mental impressions."[9]

Historical maps and atlases began to appear in the late seventeenth century, just in time to "serve history as a new intellectual discipline."[10] Examples of this early historical cartography were published in primitive textbooks in the second quarter of the nineteenth century. In 1877, Friedrich Wilhelm Putzger published his first *Historischer Schulatlas* (Historical School Atlas) of western civilization in Leipzig, Germany. It was priced at only a mark and a half so it would be easily affordable to students and others. Over a century later, the now famous Putzger atlases are still being published at reasonable prices.[11] Francis Walker's statistical maps, published in the Census Bureau's *Statistical Atlas* of 1874, marked the first attempt in the United States to convey dry statistical information in a lively and innovative way. Thematic historical maps made their way into American history textbooks in the 1880s, providing, as historian Edward Eggleston has said, "a geographical body to an historical soul."[12] Harvard University professor Albert Bushnell Hart published his "protoatlas of American history," *Epoch Maps Illustrating American History*, in 1890, and although it was inferior to Putzger's atlas in breadth of subject matter and technical use of color, it nevertheless had a major impact. Hart also published a series of classroom wall maps with Denoyer Geppert & Co. of Chicago and in 1918, with University of California professor Herbert E. Bolton, edited the *American History Atlas: Reproductions of Large Wall Maps* for the same company. Thereafter, many others, working for now famous American map publishers like Rand McNally and C. S. Hammond and Company, followed suit, their efforts culminating in 1932 with Charles O. Paullin and John K. Wright's monumental *Atlas of Historical Geography of the United States*.[13] Today historians have a great variety of maps to aid in research, writing, and teaching.

Cartographic representations, if understood in their complexity, can be used in diverse ways to teach history, but before they can be employed successfully, students must master them as both artifacts and "message images." Although historians generally regard maps, especially old ones, fundamentally as artifacts, we can appreciate maps fully only by grasping the nature of their imagery. Maps are "message images," those unique impressions formed in the mind at the time of actual viewing. As the schema reveals, "message images" are distorted before and during transmission and again upon reception and conversion into new "instant images."

Observed scene → instant images → recalled images → message images → received message conversion (new instant images)[14]

But the distortions are not necessarily deliberate or premeditated. Maps represent singular or composite "recalled images" and include subjective and even imaginative elements. According to A. G. Hodgkiss, "A map is a form of graphic communication [designed] to convey information about the environment. It provides a scaled-down view of reality extending the observer's range of vision so that he sees before him a picture of a portion, perhaps a large portion or even the whole, of the earth's surface (or of some celestial body, for not all maps are earthbound)."[15] As artifacts, then, maps extend our "range of vision" into the past; helping us observe the world as earlier people did, they improve our understanding of the thinking that shaped historic events.

The mental images portrayed in maps are of prime importance in the study of history and geography. In a new environment, such as the American frontier, what people saw was not always as important in determining their reactions to that environment as what they thought they saw or what they wanted to see. "Mental images" qualified the perception of that environment even after they had been shown to be imaginary, and real maps, showing the New World as Cathay, California as an island, the Seven Cities of Cibola, or the Northwest Passage also created and perpetuated illusions. As J. Wreford Watson explained, "Men stick by illusions based on mental abstractions, made according to pre-existing modes of thought even when their perception finally forces them to draw maps that proved them wrong: they simply transfer the illusions to other, analogous situations and press on. *The power of illusion is a major factor in the making of geography.*"[16] History is the past as

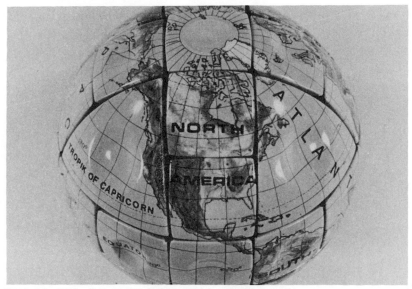

"Rubik's Globe," 1983. Collection of the author.

Herman Moll, "The Isle of California, New Mexico, Louisiane, the River Misisipi, and the Lakes of Canada," *Atlas Manuale* (London, 1713). Collection of the author.

historians interpret it, and geography is the environment as portrayed by geographers. As Watson put it, "The mental image is the environment we go by"[17] Maps are then sophisticated artifacts of history—the "eloquent documents that are well nigh indispensable sources."[18]

Thomas Jefferson, himself a cartographer, once pointed out that "a map can give a better idea of a region than any description in writing."[19] The historian of early American discovery, J. H. Parry, wrote that "topography and chronology go hand in hand, and maps are indispensable sources."[20] Maps often are the only expression of historical information, particularly for early peoples or so-called primitive human communities. Sometimes maps are the only surviving documents concerning a specific historic phenomenon, as with the notorious and highly romanticized but rarely seen treasure maps.[21]

Despite the existence of other documentary evidence, maps frequently are the most adequate source for information on discoveries and exploration, national and local boundary changes, land ownership, and land use variation. One of the most fascinating examples of the importance of maps in the history of discovery, exploration, and settlement concerns the boundary between Spanish and French North America in present-day East Texas. During the era of American discovery and exploration, topographical information was commonly treated as a state secret, especially with the reportedly treasure-rich Spanish New World. Well into the first half of the eighteenth century, French and other non-Spanish European cartographers put a large part of Spanish Texas, from the Red River to the Rio Grande, into French Louisiana on their maps. This distortion probably was based on the maps of Vincenzo Maria Coronelli, "the Cosmographer of the Venetian Republic," who also worked for King Louis XIV of France. Coronelli's distortion in turn derived from misinformation about explorations by La Salle, who had built a fort on present-day Matagorda Bay. European cartographers like Herman Moll in Great Britain updated and enhanced these distorted maps, for the Spanish maps of the area in dispute generally did not exist or were unavailable.[22] Quite a furor—a cartographic battle of the bulge—ensued in this era of early nationalism, and to

Nicolas Sanson, "Amerique Septentrionale," Paris, 1650. Cartographic History Library, University of Texas at Arlington.

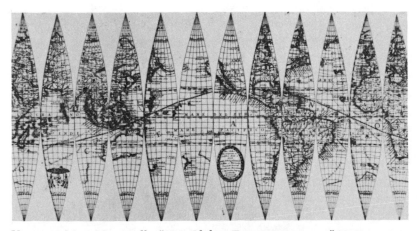

Vincenzo Maria Coronelli, "Hos Globos Terraqueum . . . ," Venice, 1693. Cartographic History Library, University of Texas at Arlington.

correct the situation, Spain was forced into a vigorous new program of exploration and mapping and into making public cartographic information about the American Southwest.

Cartographic distortions are not always the result of faulty knowledge or craftsmanship. Contemporary Soviet maps of the Soviet Union usually contain an intentional distortion of up to fifty kilometers in depicting place locations, so that in future conflicts they cannot be used effectively against the Soviet Union as were previous maps in wars dating back to Napoleon's invasion. Intentional cartographic distortions are often keys to understanding political and economic history, as in the Guatamalan-Belize territorial dispute and the British-Argentinian Falklands (Malvinas) Islands conflict.[23]

Important as well, and closely related to the study of map content, is contextual analysis. Formally putting maps into their historical perspective can be invaluable; for example, a great deal can be learned from accurately determinating creators' identities, intended audiences, and the purposes of cartographic representations. Two cases in point are sixteenth- and seventeenth-century Dutch world atlases and nineteenth-century immigrant maps of the American West.

In the sixteenth and seventeenth centuries, the vigorous bourgeois Dutch dominated much of world trade and exploration with their fleet of approximately 16,000 ships (out of a probable European total of 10,000 vessels).[24] The deeds of Henry Hudson, Abel Tasman, Peter Stuyvesant, Jan Coen, and others are well known and comprise a major chapter in the history of discovery and exploration. The works of cartographers like the Mercators, Abraham Ortelius, and the Blaeus reflected the new dominance, outlook, wealth, and values of their clientele. Their maps and atlases were sought after not only for information but also out of patriotic pride and as works of art.

Somewhat differently, the immigrant maps—be they of the vast open spaces of the American frontier, real or projected settlements, or dream cities—usually provided a combination of needed data and propaganda.[25] They were intended not only to guide travelers to their eventual destinations but also to lure them there. In fact, immigrants often were tempted by the very vagueness of

Guillaume Delisle, "Carte de la Louisiane et du Cours du Mississipi . . . ," Paris, 1718. Cartographic History Library, University of Texas at Arlington.

maps, and information about potential new homesites often was colored liberally by boosterism.

In their form as well as content, maps attest to the scientific and technological attainments of their makers. They are mathematical statements dependent upon calculations from celestial data. So, as with the schematic "T-O" maps of the Western Middle Ages depicting "Christian topography" or the Ptolemaic maps from the Renaissance, the "science" of particular maps can reveal something of the geographic and philosophical world view of the eras in which they were created. Similarly, understanding how maps are made can be very enlightening to historians and their students. Initially, maps are drawn from mental images, compiled surveys, or measurements of varying degrees of sophistication. Should they go beyond the hand-drawn or manuscript form of reproduction to multiple mechanically produced copies, then knowledge of engraving (whether on woodblocks or copperplates), lithography, and perhaps even photography is indispensable. Nor should the materials of which maps are reproduced be neglected. Whether a map is on wood, stone, clay, papyrus, vellum, paper, or plastic, studying its pigmentation and inks can disclose much about its historical context and even its validity as an historical artifact.[26] A case in point is that of the now infamous Vinland Map. Donated to Yale University in 1965 by an anonymous benefactor, it depicted North America (Vinland) as discovered by Leif Ericson in A.D. 1000. After extensive study and testing, experts judged the Vinland Map to date from about 1440, a half century before Columbus's first voyage, thereby providing documentary evidence that the Vikings discovered North America. Yale subsequently published ten thousand copies of this "most exciting cartographic discovery of the century" until conclusive tests of its ink, conducted in 1974, exposed it as a modern forgery on Renaissance paper.[27]

Maps, the products of science and technology, can also be experienced for their beauty and appeal as works of art.[28] Ultimately, like all works of art, they can be reduced to hue, line, form, and design, "a dynamic expression of color and shape" as Rudolf Arnheim has observed. Maps provide a "luxurious enrichment" of geographical and historical information; their iconic images and graphic analogies bring forth pictures from the viewer's memory. The aesthetic appeal of maps is like that of paintings that encourage the viewer to say, "Tell me who you are and what you are like."[29]

Maps create a healthy attitude of inquiry, similar to the one history educators encourage in their students. The aesthetic properties of maps invite examination, and the map as art provides "a vehicle for learning." Sensory communication is the opening gambit of the teaching-learning process and represents "the direct impact of perceptive forces." What takes place is more than a mere transmission of facts; it is the creation of a meaningful learning experience.[30]

For students this can occur on several levels. Sometimes cartographic display is the best method of conveying data: a contemporary classroom globe of the earth or topographic and thematic maps of the United States can be effective instruments of communication. Modern topographical, thematic, or historical maps usually merely illustrate in graphic form what is already well known from other sources, yet, like mathematics and music, graphic communication is an international language. Graphics are "instruments for reasoning" about information; they describe, explore, and summarize simply and powerfully. Maps, especially thematic maps, can carry a large volume of data and can stimulate a great deal of thought. As I have argued elsewhere, "No other method for the display of statistical information is so powerful."[31] Considering maps as artifacts also allows students to experience the aesthetic values of the historical contexts that produced them; a Baroque map, for example, mirrors the values of the seventeenth- and eighteenth-century Age of the Baroque.[32] Finally, maps, like other works of art, help viewers develop their own aesthetic sensibilities.

Maps also share with other works of art the characteristic of being interpretations rather than copies of reality. This has consequences for their study as historical artifacts. Map views are distortions, even with the compensation of projection, and therefore are well suited to critical analysis in the classroom. Although maps are often taken as absolute truth, they are only interpretations that are open to question. Like the Vinland Map, they can be controversial, and students can develop reasoning and research skills through analysis of cartographic documentary sources. In the process, students can also perform semantic analysis, study hermeneutics, and consider issues of historical objectivity.[33] Somewhat startling revelations often are forthcoming as, for example, when students begin to see that the apparent authority of the printed source over the manuscript source is not always warranted. Printed maps usually are simplified during translation from their sources and thus can be incorrect. Similarly, during compilation or editing, sources frequently lose some of the rich natural flavor and detail that make history what Walter Prescott Webb referred to as "high adventure."

When used as basic or supplemental instructional tools to teach the critical evaluation of evidence, maps encourage inductive reasoning, but they also can stimulate deductive reasoning when they are employed descriptively. Historians most commonly use maps for their informational content, as descriptive evidence; Walter Webb did this in his monumental *The Great Plains*. In the teaching-learning process, maps are excellent vehicles for the display of information; the concrete symbols of cartography are sometimes easier for poorer readers to comprehend than the more abstract symbols of language.[34] Maps also can demonstrate that spatial relationships are as historically significant as chronological or other relationships. For these purposes old or new maps and even especially designed historical and other thematic maps are appropriate.

Since most historians and teachers of history use maps mainly for their content, good facsimile reproductions are generally sufficient.[35] But sometimes teachers also can find originals helpful. Authentic old maps are conducive to "hands-on" education: the experience of actually holding original cartographic documents with the authority and mystique of Columbus's 1494 "First Map of America" or Stephen F. Austin's 1830 "Map of Texas" can be somewhat awesome and may encourage students to participate more intimately in the subject matter.

Use of facsimile or original maps emphasizes visual education and by sharpening visual perception, heightens the development of students' graphicacy.[36] Like literacy and numeracy, graphicacy is essential for full productive participation in modern society, where individuals are confronted daily by maps, graphs, charts, and diagrams in such indispensable and inescapable forms as road maps and signs, media news, weather and business reports, and advertising. Graphicacy is also a fundamental of computer literacy.[37]

As we have seen, maps tap the very core of the humanities and social sciences, and they can be immensely useful in the study and teaching of history. We also have seen that maps are by their complex nature multidisciplinary; they demonstrate the linkages between the sciences, social sciences, humanities, and arts, and the unity of all knowledge in human development. Although the methodology explored here is not new, there is surprisingly little in humanities, social sciences, or education literature about the use of maps specifically and artifacts generally in the teaching of history, especially in higher education.

Such a strategy nevertheless emerges as an attractive model to be incorporated into existing as well as future university courses. The artifacts do not necessarily have to be maps; they can be examples of pottery, tools, weapons, dress, medals, coins, or numerous other objects of historical significance that are readily available from museums, libraries, historical societies, corporations, and pri-

Abraham Ortelius, "Americae Siv Novi Orbis Nova Descriptio . . . ," Amsterdam, 1570. Cartographic History Library, University of Texas at Arlington.

John Disturnell, "Mapa de los Estados Unidos de Méjico . . . ," 1847. Cartographic History Library, University of Texas at Arlington.

vate collections. Knowledgeable people can explain some of the artifacts unfamiliar to the educator and can even be artifactual witnesses to contemporary events or to the distant and exotic places and happenings often depicted on maps. In order to achieve greater effectiveness, the approach can be tailored to the specific preparation and inclination of the instructor and to specific local situations. It also lends itself well to the innovative and trenchant testing of students, the culmination of the teaching-learning process. For example, given an actual map or reproduction or shown a slide thereof, students eventually can extract a great deal about the civilization, nation, and epoch of which it is an artifact.[38]

This strategy provides a respite from the didactic approach so commonly used in postsecondary institutions. In addition, it assists in diagnosing strengths and weaknesses in teaching, thus serving in part as a prescriptive tool for improvement. But the employment of maps or other artifacts in the teaching of history is not a general panacea for the teaching-learning process.[39] Maps provide stimulus variation and work best when melded with a diversity of other techniques. As a recent research study points out, maps and other artifacts "should be employed as an integral part of the social studies program. Clearly, they should not be brought in as an extra attraction in the form of 'show and tell.' Instead, they should be used as sources of data for formulating concepts and for bringing life and reality to the social studies classroom."[40]

NOTES

1. For aiding me with a major part of the research for this lecture-essay, I acknowledge my indebtedness and extend my grateful thanks to the director, Dr. Charles Colley, and the staff of the Cartographic History Library of the University of Texas at Arlington. I also would like to thank Mr. and Mrs. Jenkins Garrett for giving me full access to their extensive private map collection.

2. For example, see Malcolm G. Lewis, "The Indigenous Maps and Mapping of American Indians," *Map Collector* 9 (1979): 25–32; Louis Devorsey, "Amerindian Contributions to the Mapping of North America: A Preliminary View," *Imago Mundi* 30 (1978): 71–78; William Davenport, "Marshall Islands Navigational Charts," *Imago Mundi* 15 (1960): 19–26; H. de Hutorowicz, "Maps of Primitive Peoples," *American Geographical Society Bulletin* 43 (1911): 669–79, among others.

3. George Kish, ed. *History of Cartography* (New York: Harper and Row, 1973), slide − 1.

4. Ibid., slide −210.

5. For some good general studies of the history of cartography, see Leo Bagrow and R. A. Skelton, *History of Cartography* (Cambridge, Mass.: Harvard University Press, 1964); Lloyd A. Brown, *The Story of Maps* (New York: Dover Publications, 1980); Norman J. W. Thrower, *Maps and Man: An Examination of Cartography in Relation to Culture and Civilization* (Englewood Cliffs, N.J.: Prentice-Hall, 1976); and John Noble Wilford, *The Mapmakers* (New York: Alfred A. Knopf, 1981), among others.

6. Michael and Susan Southworth, *Maps: A Visual Survey and Design Guide* (Boston: Little, Brown and Company, 1982), 12.

7. Gillian Hill, *Cartographical Curiosities* (London: British Library, 1978), 6−20.

8. *At Last—Pier 1 by Post: Pier 1 Imports* (Fort Worth: Pier 1 Imports, 1983), 27.

9. Hill, *Cartographical Curiosities*, 18−19.

10. Lester J. Cappon, "Review Article: The Historical Maps in American Atlases," *Annals of the Association of American Geographers* 69 (December, 1979): 623. For a good early example of a historical atlas, see Herman Moll, *Thirty New and Accurate Maps of the Geography of the Ancients* . . . (London, 1726).

11. See Armin Wolf, "100 Jahre Putzger—100 Jahre Geschichtsbild in Deutschland (1877–1977)" (100 Years of Putzger—100 Years of Historical Maps in Germany (1877–1977)), *Geschichte in Wissenschaft und Unterricht* 29 (1978): 702–18.

12. Edward Eggleston, *History of the United States and Its People for the Use of Schools* (New York: D. Appleton & Co., 1888), 627. Eggleston sometimes is referred to as "the historian of the new Americans" because his books were used extensively until the 1930s to educate immigrants about the history of their new country as they studied to become American citizens.

13. Cappon, "Review Article," 623–33.

14. Judith A. Tyner, "Images of the Southwest in Nineteenth-Century American Atlases," paper presented at a symposium on the mapping of the American Southwest, the University of Texas at Arlington, February 9, 1983.

15. A. G. Hodgkiss, *Understanding Maps: A Systematic History of Their Use and Development* (Kent, England: Wm. Dawson & Son, 1981), 11.

16. J. Wreford Watson, *Mental Images and Geographical Reality in the Settlement of North America* (University of Nottingham: Cust Foundation Lecture, 1967), 3–4.

17. Ibid., 8.

18. Frank Freidel, ed., *Harvard Guide to American History* (Cambridge, Mass.: Harvard University Press, 1975), 1: 44.

19. Thomas Jefferson, *Notes on the State of Virginia*, ed. William Peden (Chapel Hill: University of North Carolina Press, 1955), 5.

20. J. H. Parry, "Old Maps Are Slippery Witnesses," *Harvard Magazine* (April, 1976): 32.

21. C. Koeman, "Levels of Historical Evidence in Early Maps," *Imago Mundi* 22 (1968): 75–78; Robert Sidney Martin and James C. Martin, eds., *Contours of Discovery: Printed Maps Delineating the Texas and Southwestern Chapters in the Cartographic History of North America (1513–1930)* (Austin: Texas State Historical Association, 1980–81), 3–4.

22. For example, see Herman Moll, "A New and Exact Map of the Dominions

of the King of Great Britain on ye Continent of North America . . ." and ". . . North America . . . ," *The World Described* . . . (London, 1715–54, and Dublin, 1730–41).

23. Koeman, "Levels of Historical Evidence,", 78; Martin and Martin, *Contours of Discovery*, 3–4; Parry, "Old Maps Are Slippery Witnesses," 32–41.

24. Jill Lisk, *The Struggle for Supremacy in the Baltic, 1600–1725* (New York: Funk and Wagnalls, 1967), 18.

25. For example, see James Wright, "Chicago . . . , 1834," in National Archives, Washington, D.C.

26. See David Woodward, ed., *Five Centuries of Map Printing* (Chicago: University of Chicago Press, 1975), and *The All-American Map: Wax Engraving and Its Influence on Cartography* (Chicago: University of Chicago Press, 1977).

27. See R. A. Skelton, Thomas E. Marston, and George D. Painter, *The Vinland Map and the Tarter Relation* (New Haven: Yale University Press, 1965). See also Michael Knight, "Yale Says Prized 'Vinland Map' of North America Is a Forgery," *New York Times*, January 26, 1974, 1.

28. For further information on this very interesting and important aspect of the history of cartography, see Henry Cayle, "On the Colouring of Maps," *Proceedings of the Royal Geographical Society* 1 (1879): 259–61; R. A. Skelton, "Colour in Mapmaking," *Geographical Magazine* 32 (1960): 544–53; R. A. Skelton, "Decoration and Design in Maps before 1700," *Graphis* 7 (1951): 400–13; and R. A. Skelton, *Decorative Printed Maps of the 15th to 18th Centuries* (London: Staple Press, 1952).

29. Rudolf Arnheim, "The Perception of Maps," *American Cartographer* 3 (1976): 5–6.

30. Ibid., 6–7.

31. Dennis Reinhartz, "The Remapping of Civilization: An Artifactual Approach to Teaching World History," *Proceedings of the Sixth International Conference on Improving University Teaching on July 9–12, 1980, in Lausanne, Switzerland* (College Park: University of Maryland, 1980), 911–12.

32. Edward R. Tufte, *The Visual Display of Quantitative Information* (Chesire, Conn.: Graphic Press, 1983), 9–26.

33. Arnheim, "The Perception of Maps," 10; Hodgkiss, *Understanding Maps*, 12; Edward C. Martin and Martin W. Sandler, "Rejuvenating the Teaching of United States History," *Social Education* 7 (1971): 733–37, 739; and Edmond T. Parker and Michael P. Conzen, *Using Maps as Evidence: Lessons in American Social and Economic History* (Bethesda, Md.: ERIC Document Reproduction Service, ED 125 935, 1975), 2.

34. Martin and Sandler, "Rejuvenating the Teaching of United States History," 737; Parker and Conzen, *Using Maps as Evidence*, 2–3.

35. Parry, "Old Maps Are Slippery Witnesses," 41.

36. Parker and Conzen, *Using Maps as Evidence*, 2.

37. See Tufte, *The Visual Display of Quantitative Information*.

38. Reinhartz, "The Remapping of Civilization," 913–14.

39. Jane J. Anderson, "Teaching History by the Audio–Tutorial Method," *History Teacher* 3 (1969): 36–41; Martin and Sandler, "Rejuvenating the Teaching of United States History," 739; and Parker and Conzen, *Using Maps as Evidence*, 2.

40. Janet Alleman-Brooks, Ambrose A. Clegg, Jr., and Albert P. Sebolt, "Making the Past Come Alive," *Social Studies* 68 (*January–February, 1977*): 6.

Selected Cartographic Resources for Teaching History with Maps

Books:

Bagrow, Leo, and R. A. Skelton. *History of Cartography*. Cambridge, Mass.: Harvard University Press, 1964.

Brown, Lloyd A. *The Story of Maps*. New York: Dover Publications, 1977.

Campbell, Tony. *Early Maps*. New York: Abbeville Press, 1981.

Hill, Gillian. *Cartographical Curiosities*. London: British Library, 1978.

Martin, James C., and Robert Sidney Martin. *Maps of Texas & the Southwest, 1513–1900*. Albuquerque: University of New Mexico Press, 1984.

Nordensköld, A. E. *Facsimile-Atlas to the Early History of Cartography with Reproductions of the Most Important Maps Printed in the XV and XVI Centuries*. New York: Dover Publications, 1973.

Post, J. B. *An Atlas of Fantasy*. London: Souvenir Press, 1979.

Putnam, Robert. *Early Sea Charts*. New York: Abbeville Press, 1983.

Schwartz, Seymour, and Ralph E. Ehrenberg. *The Mapping of America*. New York: Harry N. Abrams, 1980.

Skelton, R. A. *Maps: A Historical Survey of Their Study and Collecting*. Chicago: University of Chicago Press, 1975.

Southworth, Michael, and Susan Southworth. *Maps: A Visual Survey and Design Guide*. Boston: Little, Brown and Company, 1982.

Thrower, Norman J. W. *Maps and Man: An Examination of Cartography in Relation to Culture and Civilization*. Englewood Cliffs, N.J.: Prentice-Hall, 1976.

Wilford, John Noble. *The Mapmakers*. New York: Alfred A. Knopf, 1981.

Woodward, David. *Five Centuries of Map Printing*. Chicago: University of Chicago Press, 1975.

Facsimile reproductions:

Martin, Robert Sidney, and James C. Martin. *Contours of Discovery: Printed Maps Delineating the Texas and Southwestern Chapters in the Cartographic History of North America*. Austin: Texas State Historical Association, 1981–82. 22 maps.

Historic Urban Plans
Box 276
Ithaca, New York 14850

Journals and regular publications:

Imago Mundi. Journal of the International Society for the History of Cartography. Lympne Castle, Kent, England.

The Map Collector. Tring: Map Collector Publications, Ltd. P.O. Box 53, Tring, Herts, England HP23 5BH.

Mapline. Hermon Dunlap Smith Center for the History of Cartography. The Newberry Library, 60 W. Walton Street, Chicago, Illinois 60610.

Terrae Incognitae. Journal of the Society for the History of Discoveries. Barbara McCorkle, Secretary-Treasurer, 45 Mill Rock Road, Hamden, Conn. 06511.

Slide sets:

Kish, George. *The Discovery and Settlement of North America, 1500–1865: A Cartographic Perspective*. New York: Harper and Row, Publishers, 1978. 203 slides and cassette tape.

————. *History of Cartography*. New York: Harper and Row, Publishers, 1973. 220 slides.

Sources for Historical thematic maps and atlases:
Hammond Incorporated
515 Valley Street
Maplewood, N.J. 07040
For historical atlases—Penguin Books
                    625 Madison Avenue
                    New York, N.Y. 10022
For historical map transparency sets—Gould Media, Inc.
                    44 Parkway West
                    Mount Vernon, N.Y. 10552
For revolutions and wars atlases—Simon & Schuster
                    Rockefeller Center
                    1230 Avenue of the Americas
                    New York, N.Y. 10020

Postscript: Some Thoughts and Comments on Walter Prescott Webb as Teacher

How varied are the institutions that might exhibit a plaque with the words: "Walter Prescott Webb taught here." He had taught at Barnet School, Cedar Point, and Mountain School in Eastland County before he graduated from Ranger High School in 1908. Then came a term of teaching at Merriman before entering the University of Texas at Austin in the fall of 1909. After two years at the university, he taught a year at Brushy Knob in Throckmorton County, then went back to the university for the B.A. degree. He taught at Beeville in 1913, had varied assignments at Southwest Texas State Normal School at San Marcos, and worked stints at Cuero and San Antonio High Schools prior to joining the history department of the University of Texas to teach a course for prospective history teachers in Texas public schools. In 1916 he attended summer school at the University of Wisconsin. He had his M.A. degree from the University of Texas and spent an unhappy year at the University of Chicago without completing a dissertation for the doctorate. (His first important book, *The Great Plains*, was accepted by the University of Texas history department as his dissertation.) Webb's long tenure at the University of Texas history department was interspersed with summer teaching at the University of Wyoming, Harvard, Duke, and West Virginia. In 1938 he was Harkness Professor at the University of London, and 1942 found him back in England as Harmsworth Professor at Oxford.

Clarence Ayres, memorializing Webb in the University of Texas *Graduate Journal* in the winter of 1964, wrote: "I still know him and honor him, and profit by him. Nothing can alter what he has done and what he has been, and I shall always be proud to be one of the many whose lives have been touched by him." Eleven years later *New York Times* of January 5, 1975, carried an editorial called "Vanishing Frontier," which concluded: "The frontier has vanished. There is no empty land in which to escape. People have to live within nature's constraints or suffer from the consequences." The boom that lasted for four and a half centuries had meant "appreciation of the individual, self-motivation, capitalism and democracy." Walter Prescott Webb had been thirty years ahead of his time in foreseeing that society was to go through a process of "devolution and retrogression."

In 1931, when he completed his first great book, Webb inscribed a copy of *The Great Plains* to the teacher who had most impressed him:

> To Dr. Lindley Miller Keasbey
> Thinker and Teacher
> Where others gave information he gave a point of view, a method, and a power to think constructively; by example, as well as by precept, he gave courage to think independently. His influence has permeated but never bound what I have done and is present in the whole fabric of this work. The book is presented as a belated expression of the gratitude and affection of the writer.
> Walter Prescott Webb
>
> Austin
> September 18, 1931

It was ten years later that Webb wrote an editorial for the *Junior Historian*, the magazine for students of high school history. The number for September, 1941, emphasized the "Function of History" as follows: "History is the invoice of a bill of goods acquired by purchase and inheritance from the past and offered to man in the market of the immediate and distant future. . . . History is the papers of man; it is the register of his lineage, the record of his performance, and the guarantee of his qualities."

Webb's last speech was made to the Retired Teachers Association in San Antonio. To those colleagues he said that he took teaching as a vocation and writing as an avocation. He felt an obligation to his students, and he considered teaching as a profession "no more honorable and no less than any honest way of making a living." He disclaimed wanting disciples because he never wanted to be one but wanted to think for himself and have his students do the same. One of Webb's students, Stephen Oates, quoted Webb as saying that "books themselves are only keys which admit us into the various rooms of the mansion of real living."

Jubal Parten, in his foreword to Volume X of the *Webb Memorial Letters*, stated of Webb: "As a teacher, he was deeply concerned that the student be exposed to the best teaching from the standpoint of both quality and content." Parten emphasized Webb's prophetic vision in *The Great Frontier*, with its brilliant comprehension of the world we are living in today. The last words of that Webb opus were: "Our challenge consists in finding out what modifications should be made, and our opportunity will come in making them. Our inspiration may come from history in looking back to the early sixteenth century when the lamp was lifted beside the golden door of the Great Frontier to change the destiny of mankind."

In 1959 Webb spoke at the inauguration of Ralph Steen as president of Stephen F. Austin University and was introduced as "a master teacher." After Webb's death, his eulogies were varied. Arnold Toynbee extolled him for his "point of view," a vision that became global. He wrote that Webb managed to "combine the mastery of a special area of history with a vision of the total history of the world." C. Vann Woodward described Webb as the incarnation of his own environmentalist doctrine, one who was endeared to his fellow craftsmen "by his dedication to his subject and the enthusiasm with which he pursued it." In a special Webb section of *Graduate Journal*, Al Burdine used a variety of superlatives for Webb: an entertaining conversationalist, a great storyteller, a hard-nosed adviser, "a person of integrity, courage, and inimitable wit." Clarence Ayres admired Webb for his moral courage in writing *Divided We Stand* and *The Great Frontier*, "the moral of which we are doomed to witness."

In 1969 William Owens wrote of the three friends, Webb, Dobie, and Bedichek, describing Webb as his most ideal teacher. Walter Rundell, writing of Webb the teacher, describes Webb's intellectual journey as a "most unusual circuit for one who became a master of his craft. As the years and honors mounted, he became less the traditional historian and more the writer-artist."